AT THE EDGE OF HISTORY

AT THE EDGE
OF HISTORY

William Irwin Thompson

HARPER TORCHBOOKS
Harper & Row, Publishers
New York, Hagerstown, San Francisco, London

Permission granted by the following publishers for use of material under copyright is gratefully acknowledged: For Chapter 1, which first appeared as "Los Angeles: Reflections at the Edge of History," *The Antioch Review,* Vol. XXVIII, No. 3, September, 1968 (Copyright, 1968). For lines from T. S. Eliot's "Little Gidding" *Four Quartets* (Copyright, 1943, T. S. Eliot), Harcourt Brace Jovanovich. For lines from W. C. Williams' "The Pink Church," *The Collected Later Poems* (Copyright, 1949, W. C. Williams), New Directions. For a selection from *Symbolism in Religion and Literature,* edited by Rollo May (Copyright, 1960, George Braziller, Inc. and Copyright, 1958, by the American Academy of Arts and Sciences). For lines from W. B. Yeats's "A Dialogue of Self and Soul" and "The Supernatural Songs," *Collected Poems,* The Macmillan Company (Copyright, 1934; renewed by Bertha Georgie Yeats, 1962). For selections from "Toward the Year 2000," edited by Daniel Bell, *Daedalus,* Vol. 96, No. 3 (Summer, 1967), American Academy of Arts and Sciences. For selections from *Psychoanalysis and the Unconscious* by D. H. Lawrence (Copyright, 1921, by Thomas Seltzer, Inc., renewed 1949 by Frieda Lawrence, reprinted by permission of The Viking Press, Inc.). For selections from *The Year 2000: A Framework for Speculation on the Next Thirty-Three Years* by Herman Kahn and Anthony Weiner, The Macmillan Company (Copyright, 1967, Herman Kahn and Anthony Weiner).

First HARPER TORCHBOOK edition published 1979.
ISBN: 0-06-131946-5

Designed by Yvette A. Vogel

79 80 81 82 83 10 9 8 7 6 5 4 3 2 1

FOR GAIL

We shall not cease from exploration
And the end of all our exploring
Will be to arrive where we started
And know the place for the first time . . .
When the tongues of flame are in-folded
Into the crowned knot of fire
And the fire and the rose are one.

T. S. Eliot, LITTLE GIDDING

CONTENTS

PREFACE

The technology of our industrial civilization has reached a peak in putting a man on the moon, but, as the ancients knew, the peak is also the moment of descent. Before we ascend the next peak to Mars, there is a very dark valley waiting beneath us, and, poetically enough, its darkness is made up of just those things our civilization did in order to succeed. In straining our industrial technology to the limit, we have, in fact, reached the limit of that very technology. Now as we stand in the shadow of our success, there remains light enough to see that we are approaching a climax in human cultural evolution: it seems as if the whole history of earth were being played back, but speeded up.

One can say almost anything about human culture now and it will be true, for everything is going on at once: from the test-tube disappearance of sexuality in procreation to the new explosion of sexuality in creativity; from the disappearance of the nation-state to the explosion of nationalism in Quebec, Wales, Scotland, and the land of the Basques; from the appearance of a new radicalism to the resurgence of a new conservatism; from a planetary miscegenation to a new tribal racism. Yet one thing is not happening in America: we are not growing together, but are polarizing every conceivable condition to its extremes. It is as if only the energy created by the violent polarization of the old had sufficient power to drive the new evolution of man.

We cannot tell what is out there beyond the year 2000, but we can sense the power and the direction of the forces that are now playing upon us. It would seem that they are after our machines, demanding that we strip ourselves of the very *things* that have made us what we are. But what we are is not what we are about to become: the aborigines of another fall or the adepts of a new civilization beyond matter. At the edge of history the future is blowing wildly in our faces, sometimes brightening the air and sometimes blinding us. To get a sense of where we are going, I tried to see out through the geographical limits of my own experience to the spaces of our contemporary culture where the millennial imagination of the future is interrupting the daily news of the present. In those heightened moments of American anticipation and dread, the past and the future come together to shatter the prevailing order of society. At such instants, actual events appear to burst into apocalyptic liberation (Eros) or to close in totalitarian collectivization (Thanatos), and the ordinary shapelessness of historical reality is lost in new cinematic forms in which the event itself takes on the joy of sacrament and the terror of sacrifice.

In my earlier book, *The Imagination of an Insur-*

*rection,** I was concerned with the way in which
the imagination of the past impinged upon the revolutionary behavior in Ireland at the turn of the century. Here I am concerned with the other turn of
the twentieth century and the way in which our
imagination of the year 2000 is impinging on the
revolutionary behavior of contemporary America.
By setting up the two poles of our historical consciousness in the mythical past and the millennial
future, I am attempting to describe a few ways in
which the imagination of history affects society.
When a historian works within the center of the
space and time of a culture, he feels that his subject
is so immense that the importance of his work can be
taken for granted. But my position is closer to that
of the anthropologist, who works at the edge, and
for whom the description of another culture is also
the search for an alternative civilization.

Los Angeles, Boston, Toronto
1967–1970

* *The Imagination of an Insurrection: Dublin, Easter 1916*
(Oxford, 1967).

AT THE EDGE OF HISTORY

1

LOOKING FOR
HISTORY IN L.A.

At the end of the eighteenth century it was the rage
to journey to ruins and graveyards and meditate
upon the prospect these stones held out to mortal
man. Now, as the twentieth century declines, it is
the rage to journey to Los Angeles and meditate
upon the prospect that city holds out to the rest of
the nation. Unlike the gravestone, Los Angeles seems
to have become a marker of just how far we can go
and stay this side of history. As Richard M. Elman
puts it: "I went to Compton with the thought in
mind that this was the future. It is what lies in store
for all the new suburbs of all the big cities of Amer-
Ica. Southern California lends itself to this. It is,
after all, the greatest megalopolis in the most popu-
lous state in the nation."[1]* In Elman's tone of dread
is, of course, the Easterner's fear that sun-tanned
nomads are about to spring out of the Southwestern
desert and overrun civilization as he knows it. The
fear is a popular one, for in the past few years a
host of Easterners have made the journey to Los

* Notes begin on page 232.

3

Angeles to study the nature of its threat to urban civilization. All these new books and articles have contributed to our dread of things to come, but still something is missing. If one is concerned with the strange goings-on out at the edge of history, then it would seem natural that he should wonder just what the whole *idea of history* becomes for people who live at the edge.

As one who grew up in Los Angeles and as one who always wished to escape it for "a real life back east," I have become astonished to find that I cannot let go of Los Angeles even though I live away from it. Other expatriates I know from Southern California have settled into comfortably civilized lives in Boston and New York, and I would think my fascination with Los Angeles almost patholgoical were it not for the fact that so many Easterners share it. The only people more obsessed with Los Angeles than the residents themselves are the people who don't live there. If no man is an island, it would seem that in our era of urbanization he is automatically a resident of a suburb of L.A. Those expatriates from Southern California who succeed in shutting Los Angeles out of their minds do so because they are past-oriented and turning their backs on the future is a posture that comes naturally to them. They recognize the sense of dread that emanates from the city at the edge, but they hope the future will overlook them and that they will be able to make it all the way to the end of their lives undisturbed. But even in turning away from Los Angeles they reveal the rich fantasy life of the L.A. man and turn Eastern life into a caricature of fashion that proves them not to the manner born. Like Oscar Wilde, that Anglo-Irishman in a world of real Englishmen and real Irishmen, the expatriate can only achieve identity at the cost of self-distorting excess.

For those whose fantasies are about the future rather than the past, Los Angeles is an inevitable subject of speculation, if only for the simple reason that fantasy can live a richer life in the West than in the East. In the East the burden of tradition, power, and religion is so great that the fantasy has little room in which to realize itself. When the sociologist William R. Ellis came to speak about his native Watts at a symposium on Los Angeles held at M.I.T., he said that he felt that whenever he had had it with being an academic liberal Negro, he could take off his tweed coat, don robes, and go out and change the world. "Somehow or other I get the feeling that I just couldn't do that here in Boston." In Los Angeles it is much harder to distinguish between personal fantasy and social reality because the realization of fantasy is one of our dominant cultural traits—from Disneyland to Sacramento. It would be a simple matter if one could say that all fantasy is bad, and, therefore, that the East is right and the West is wrong; but like all dualistic arrangements, the human predicament seems to cut at right angles across the cosmic division between good and evil. Fantasy is good and bad, just as the lack of it is good and bad. As the psychiatrist R. D. Laing has said:

Not all psychologists know of fantasy as a modality of experience, and the, as it were, contrapuntal interweaving of different experiential modes. Many who are aware of fantasy believe that fantasy is the farthest that experience goes under "normal" circumstances. Beyond that are simply "pathological" zones of hallucinations, phantasmagoric mirages, delusions.

This state of affairs represents an almost unbelievable devastation of our experience. Then there is empty chatter about maturity, love, joy, peace.[2]

The average citizen who has escaped the dreariness of the village mentality of the South or the Midwest has encountered in Southern California the freedom to find himself, or lose himself. Most people are frightened by the possibilities of this new freedom, and as they sense themselves slipping away from the traditional American culture of work into the new culture of pleasure, they recoil from the edge and have fantasies of "the real thing" that is "just like back east." And these fantasies make the guilt they feel for their own self-indulgence easier to live with.

But these fantasies of tradition are not limited to Hollywood or Orange County. When Chancellor Dean McHenry of the new University of Santa Cruz gestured to the barren rolling hlils and said that there was to be another Amherst, another Bryn Mawr, another Swarthmore, he was demonstrating how even a university campus can turn out to be a movie set. McHenry went on to say that "There will be traditions." Friends at UCSC tell me that there are high teas and a high table.

This form of the realization of fantasy is not restricted to one sector of the Southern California way of life; it is all-pervasive. Los Angeles restaurants and their parking lots are such million-dollar structures because they are palaces of fantasy in which the upward-moving individual comes to act out a self-mythology he has learned from a hero of the mass media. Often enough the establishment of La Cienega Boulevard's Restaurant Row are fantasies of history in their very architecture. Within a few blocks one can move from an old English inn to a Tahitian hut, a Mediterranean villa, a Japanese garden, and such sentimentalizations of the past as "The Gay Nineties" and "The Roaring Twenties." On certain nights some restaurants pass out balloons, hats, and noisemakers so that the guests may fantasy that they are enjoying themselves. Disneyland is not an anomaly contained by Anaheim, but a gathering and concentration of the Southern California world view.

My own adolescent fantasy of the real thing was Ireland. Ireland was green, while Los Angeles was desert; Ireland was filled with white thatched cottages, Los Angeles with pink-stucco tract homes with Swiss chalet trim. In Ireland the devout did not keep rhinestone medals of the Virgin on their chests and push-button knives in their pockets. On my first date I took a girl named Norma O'Brien to see John Ford's *The Quiet Man,* and then went back to see it again, and again: each time wishing through the effigy of John Wayne that I might be permitted to return (as John Ford actually has) to the ancestral *Land of Heart's Desire.* What one wishes for at fourteen has a way of taking over, for years later as a graduate student I won a fellowship to Ireland and felt then that I was, at last, moving away from Hollywood to a land of historical reality. As I flew across the Atlantic in a white Boeing Aer

Lingus jet, I could not stop from thinking of the dirty and diseased immigrant steamship in which my great-grandmother had made the crossing to America a hundred years before. And the more I thought of those two family movements in time, the more I became aware that the book I wanted to write was involved with more of Irish history than 1916. The writing of the book began to represent to me the completion of a small familial cycle that in its tininess reflected the larger movements of Irish history.

The forward movement began, on my father's side, with the Ulster Scots fleeing the catastrophe of seventeenth-century Ireland to come to the farmlands of Pennsylvania; and, on my mother's side, with my great-grandmother fleeing the catastrophe of nineteenth-century Ireland to come to the Chicago of my parents. I took part in another westward movement that brought a great part of the Midwest into California at the end of the Second World War, and there, free of the containment of the urban Irish ghetto or the Midwestern farm, I could grow up transforming the taco stands and gas stations of my surroundings into the pubs and tinker camps of a *real* country. But in writing about Easter 1916 and in living in Ireland, I began to see that I had been bewildered by an excess of love in the same way that the revolutionaries had been. To be sure, my fantasies were not as great or as deadly as theirs; for me the shock of the real Ireland with its highest insanity rate in the world was simply an awakening slap in the face of my Celtic reveries. It was fitting that, in the writing of a book on imagination, my own was forced to come to terms with the reality of modern Ireland. A family cycle was completed and I was free to go back to America without the fantasy hyphenations of my former national identity.

But you cannot throw over Ireland so easily; the mythic pattern of Irish history never let go of me, and if anything was likely to strengthen its possession, it was the experience of writing about the insurrection in Dublin while my own city was going up in flames and black men were being machine-gunned in the streets of Watts in 1965. Standish O'Grady's 1899 prophecy of the revolution in Ireland now seemed to fit America as well: "We have now a literary movement, it is not very important; it will be followed by a political movement, that will not be very important; then must come a military movement, that will be very important indeed." It took seventeen years to prove O'Grady right, and that space of time seems about right for America. We had our literary movement in the fifties with the Beat movement and the folk song revival; it was followed by the political movement of civil rights and the expulsion of the white intellectuals from SNCC in the sixties; and now we are in the military movement of the Weathermen and the Black Panthers. The artists and the intellectuals are important in the literary phase of revolution, but by the time of the military movement, when the proletariat, be it Irish or black, has brought its masses to a lethal point, the scruples of the intellectuals, be they Irish Protestant or American white, are swept aside as impediments to effective mobilization. If Ireland continues to be our model, as it appears it will, then the theatrical media revolts of the poets and dreamers will be followed by the civil guerrilla urban warfare of men of a very different cast.

As I brooded over the Irish Revolution and Watts, I became aware of the irony that I had moved away from California to look for real and historically deep cultures at a time when it was California's turn to make history. The feeling of that irony grew in me even while I had to ignore it while teaching humanities at M.I.T., but in the spring of 1967 the feeling took over and turned me around in my academic place to face toward the West and the year 2000. I had been offered an Old Dominion Fellowship, supposedly to work in London, but I told myself that it was silly to labor on some piece of academic criticism at a time when history was becoming possessed with visions of an angelic and diabolic kind. America in the winter of 1966–67 seemed to be in the beginning of some huge transformation, and Ronald Reagan and the hippies were a joint persuasion that a new exchange between myth and history was taking place at the edge of America.

And so the search for history shifted from Europe to L.A., and as once again I moved against a landscape of smog-blurred air, sunburnt hills, lurid signs, gas stations, taco stands, and pink chalet tract homes made out of chicken wire and dunglike stucco, I knew I was no longer moving in a "city" in any historical sense. Historically, civilization is what goes on in cities.[3] We are only beginning to find out what goes on in a megalopolis. The people who live in Los Angeles proper, Beverly Hills, and Westwood seem to be as civilized as their counterparts in any major American city. They have bookstores, art galleries, museums, theaters, and parks for social expression. But in the vast urban sprawl the tracts of houses are only relieved by freeways and shopping centers. Orange County is the preeminent example of the new posturban landscape, and, as every paranoid Eastern liberal knows, Orange County is the capital of California Right Wing extremism. The lower-middle classes fled the South and the Midwest for the airplane-defense jobs during the war, and with Korea and the new aerospace industry they kept up the wars in their Pacific lake to keep those jobs coming They had come to Southern California for space and weather, and in the crowded, smog-infested tracts around the defense plants, they found neither, but learned to forget both in their newly acquired swimming pools and sports cars.

Now as one moves through this shattered landscape in which the mountains are invisible from the exhausts of four and a half million cars and the orange trees have been eliminated for real estate speculation, how is he to gain any sense of history except through the artificial monuments he sees nearby in Disneyland or, in the even more Right Wing Crystal Palace, Knott's Berry Farm—where Philadelphia's Independence Hall has been duplicated brick by brick? Since there is no history to be seen or experienced in any meaningful way, the citizen must grab onto time and hold on for all he is worth. He must nourish an inner fantasy landscape in which he figures larger than he does in life, or suffer the risk of losing himself utterly. It is for this reason that Southern Californians imagine ivy-covered, leaf-strewn squares, and villages clustered around white frame New England churches, and, lacking them in reality, create them in the plastic towns to which they go to find themselves.

Frivolous as all this realization of fantasy may seem, its role in the individual's consciousness (or unconsciousness) is an important aspect of his social and political behavior. A culture's idea of history is related to its present, and in Southern California the idea of history is iconically enshrined in Anaheim. The idea of history is a shattered landscape in which the indivdual moves through a world of discontinuities: Mississippi riverboats, medieval castles, and rocket ships equally fill the reality of a single moment. When children could not articulate their problems, the psychologist Erik Erikson used to observe them at play with the toys in his office; inevitably they would act out their fantasies. Disneyland is such a place. But the essential question of this Southern California idea of history is: What happens to the individual who grows up with it? What is life like for a person who moves through the shattered landscape of the megalopolis in which time, tradition, and history are scrambled? What sense of identity does the citizen have when the city he lives in is without a significant image? For the image of the city is not simply a matter of beautification; it is a matter of giving to the individual the basic ontological security of knowing where he is in life. As the city planner Kevin Lynch has remarked:

In the process of way-finding, the strategic link is the environmental image, the generalized mental picture of the exterior physical world that is held by an individ-

ual. . . . The need to recognize and pattern our surroundings is so crucial, and has such long roots in the
past, that this image has wide practical and emotional
importance to the individual.

Obviously a clear image enables one to move about
easily: to find a friend's house or a policeman or a
button store. But an ordered environment can do more
than this; it may serve as a broad frame of reference,
an organizer of activity or belief or knowledge.[4]

When the megalopolis is too vast to be perceived
meaningfully, the individual projects, against the
chaos of his world, a new mythopoeic simplification.
Whether the myth is Right Wing, Black Nationalist,
or the Cal Tech freshman's millenarian science fiction myth of space (or my own fantasy of pipe-
smoking Ivy League professors with knowledge and
wisdom shining out of their eyes), the myth is a fiery
signature of a new reality making a special covenant
with the individual. Man simply cannot tolerate the
stress of an absence of order; if the urban sprawl is
without order, he will see patterns in it even if these
patterns are paranoid signs of a conspiracy.

Oedipa Maas, the mirror image of Oedipus Rex
and the heroine of Thomas Pynchon's brilliant novella, *The Crying of Lot 49*, searches throughout
Southern California for her inheritance from her big
daddy lover, and as she becomes increasingly lost,
she begins to see the signs of the Trystero underground network of postal communication on the
trash cans of the state. She searches for an inheritance from a past that is dead, discovers an imagined
system of communication in a land where human
communications fails, and finds in the rubbish of the
state the fertile decay for her own ambiguous regen-

eration. Pynchon's profound novel is the story as well of every Southern California Right Winger who reads everywhere about him the signs of an underground Communist conspiracy, but the real tragedy of the novella comes from the fact that these caricatures also describe the scientific perception of nature. Myths are simplifications of reality, but so are scientific laws, for they magnetize the infinite information of the universe into the fields of their own formulaic descriptions; what is objectively outside the field of our consciousness is literally inconceivable. If we wish smugly to put down the imaginative perceptions of Oedipa Maas, we will also have to take apart the relationship between imagination and reality in the quantum theory of Werner Heisenberg.[5] Because mind is a contribution to reality, the more mind one has, the more he sees in reality, and madmen, poets, and physicists are all of a company apart from readers of ticker tapes and scholarly journals. In his comic parodies of knowledge in an age of data processing, Pynchon has brilliantly succeeded in relating science to the artist's vision of tragedy and human ambiguity. *The Crying of Lot 49,* like Nathanael West's *Day of the Locust* before it, is worth volumes of sociology, and in focusing on a heroine who is cut off from familial identifications, Pynchon has recognized just how the connective tissue of history breaks down at the edge.

The strongest connective tissue of history is, of course, the family and its cultural extensions in the church and temple. The ghetto mentality of South Boston or Brooklyn gives the individual definition and identity, but, satisfying as that can be, it can often be a prison. Definition can be a form of restraint in which the child is expected to marry a Catholic or a Jew, take over the shop, or not marry because Mama needs her. Traditional society can be a static one in which the individual is expected to stay put in his family, his home, his neighborhood, his religion, and often even his job. It can all be very comforting, but it can also be deadly. To someone from Los Angeles, Boston, with its Ancient Order of Hibernians and its Sons of Italy, looks like a living museum. In Los Angeles one can change his house, job, wife, and religion pretty much as he likes. If one lives in an Irish ghetto and misses Mass once, the family has the priest bearing down on him. In Los Angeles the family situation is loosened because the extended family is back wherever the nuclear family came from, and as the nuclear family grows up, it is likely to remain loose by spinning off its new families into widely separated suburban towns. But even with the nuclear family further fragmentation seems to be developing in the new pattern of life in the Southern California megalopolis, where the Eleventh Commandment is: "Thou shalt not grow old."

A slightly upper-middle-class young engineer moves into a "Singles" either before he marries or just after his first divorce. (One must remember that the divorce rate in California is twice that of the nation, or one out of every *two* marriages.) Because all his friends and acquaintances are related to his previous marriage, the young divorcé needs a place for what the developers call "interim living"—a place where he may begin a new life with new friends in a "community atmosphere." This sense of community is necessary because, more likely than not, the family that could help him over the difficult period of divorce (or intimidate him out of ever seeking one) is somewhere back in the vast expanse of the Midwest that lies behind Southern California in space and time. But if the young engineer has never married and has his twelve thousand a year and more to himself, then he is in a position to entertain, with Corvettes and Chivas Regal, the bikini-clad girls who decorate the pool of his apartment-club complex. In some "Singles," if the girls are sufficient architectural contributions to the landscaping of the pool, their rent is lower than that of the young professional men who can quite easily and willingly make up the difference. After the young engineer samples the offerings of his female neighbors, he nearly doubles his income by getting married and moving up to an accelerated phase of consumption: two cars, stereos, appliances, and perhaps a boat. When this program is stopped by the pregnancy of the wife (if this is desired, and it is not in many cases, for indebtedness can postpone pregnancy indefinitely), the engineer moves out with his wife to a tract house in a newly opened "Planned Community." And here he begins the child-bearing phase of life by joining *sub*-urban civilization.

A "Planned Community" is another new concept in real estate development like the "Singles." Rather than bulldozing the trees and putting up house after house in four basic styles, the developers now include concrete-embedded artificial lakes for boating, golf courses, swimming pools, tennis courts, teen-age clubhouses, and advertise that life becomes a per-

manent vacation when one lives in this instant community. If the extra payments over the mortgage
that one pays for all the facilities become too much,
along with all the other payments, then the wife returns to work and the children grow up in age sets
and derive their norms from their own generational
peer group. With the approach of adolescence and
the driver's license, the children have a mobility of
several hundred miles and one foreign country,
Mexico. As the children go off to one of the universities, state colleges, or local junior colleges (and
the peripheral dropout life that clusters around each
in varying degrees of hippiness), the engineer and
his wife (if it is the same wife) are free to return to the
joys of urban society. He moves back into the city
and takes up residence in a luxury condominium in
which the Minoan bathroom is a positive shrine to
the glories of the flesh that are fast slipping beyond
his middle-aged reach. Once he has tasted the nou-
veau elegance of the forty-million-dollar cultural
shopping plaza downtown at the Music Center, and
forgotten his days of Little League and Boy Scouts,
and once the frantic sexuality of the middle-age
period has quieted down, he is free to move away
from condominiums, key clubs, and topless restaurants to the retirement community of Leisure World.

But more than likely a Californian of some years'
standing could not live with all the aged Midwestern-
ers who have come to Leisure World to get in on the
California scene with the last chance they have. Not
having had the courage to get up and leave sooner,
those who have waited docilely for retirement to free
them from Ogallala and Wichita are not likely to

prove the best companions for one who has lived with his top down all his life. But for those who have come to Leisure World from the traditional ways of American life, a room in the two-story, three-generational home in a small town will never seem better than Leisure World. With bowling green, swimming pool, hobby rooms, closed-circuit TV station, classes, shops and regular meetings of the Kansas Club, guilt-ridden immigrants to this new world can indulge their fantasies by talking about the good old days in another country.

The effect of this new pattern of life is to separate in space and time within the megalopolis the critical periods of life. No longer need a person carry the burden of a single identity from the cradle to the grave. He is free to change lives and wives as often as he has the energy. I imagine that the way McLuhan would describe this pattern is that the individual is no longer a novel, but a television set: at the flip of a channel he changes his program. Disneyland itself is a kind of television set, for one flips from medieval castles to submarines and rockets as easily as one can move, in downtown Los Angeles, from the plaza of the Mexican Olvera Street to Little Tokyo, to the modern Civic Center with its new pavilion for the performing arts.

But these discontinuities of history are no longer to be contained by Disneyland and Southern California. As the SST jet brings us closer to what the city planner Constantinos Doxiadis calls "Ecumenopolis," the Los Angelization of the past becomes quite possible. Even now as one looks out of the window of his Boeing 720 on the L.A.-to-Boston run, it seems as if he were flipping channels on a continental TV set: California tracts, Southwestern desert, a drink, and then it's Rocky Mountains, Green Iowa, the Finger Lakes, the Hudson, and then back, in time as well as space, to Boston. In the old days the difficulty of travel preserved the integrity of widely separated cultures. Now the cultures are being scrambled together, and the traditions of the fathers seem irrelevant to the lives of the sons, whether the sons are in Watts, Vietnam, or Nigeria. What Los Angeles is experiencing is the future for us all. The violent juxtaposition of aerospace technology and neo-tribal politics contains the thesis and antithesis of the new planetary culture; hopefully, the synthesis will be contained in the coming twenty-first century.

In the meantime more people will lose their way than find themselves in this new world. As they become lost, they will fall into the artificial subcultures of Right Wing Americanism, Black Nationalism, Maoism, hippiedom, and the cults of the flying saucer contactees. Lacking the strong connective tissue of tradition, the individual can entertain in his fantasy life various possible identities. Since nothing is to stop him from acting out his fantasies, he can flip from identity to new identity, changing jobs and communities, as he makes his odyssey through the vast Mediterranean world of Southern California. Since one lives in generational ghettos, there is no continuity in generational exchanges of knowledge. There is only the community of those who share one's historical moment, for these are the only ones who can be trusted to be a genuine part of one's world. The young mother in a new tract may find that the average age of her entire neighborhood is under thirty. She will find many other pregnant wives to talk with, but she will not find any older "Jewish mothers" to give her a larger kind of sympathy.

Living in a generational ghetto becomes like living on a campus where there are no teachers other than one's fellow students. Since all too often the best teachers are one's fellow students, this is not necessarily for the worst. There is a good deal more wisdom in Bob Dylan than in Robert Welch. Nevertheless, this new discontinuous life-rhythm helps traditional wisdom to disappear; which means that, negatively, the young are doomed to repeat history because they are ignorant of it; and, positively, that the young can react more quickly to the accelerated process of technological change. The imaginations of the older generation are bogged down by the economic and technical arrangements of a previous epoch. The members of the older generation are like the land-owners of Attica who did not want Themistocles to use the surplus from the silver mines to finance the building of an Athenian navy; their feudal imaginations could not understand the new capitalism that Themistocles' Athenian Empire held out to them.

Precisely because the California Miracle was made by government intervention into the private sector through the railroads, the defense industries, and FHA housing, our elders from the Old World have become frightened at the prospects of the metacapitalistic, technological society and have regressed into a caricatured version of the past. Precisely because there is no real tradition, the elders create fantasies of mother, country, God (who is really Uncle Sam in more heavenly attire), private property, flag and family, and on and on in the litany of the atavist. Significantly, the entrance to Disneyland is through a nostalgic, garter-sleeved, soda-fountained, marble-topped, apothecary-jarred small town. The small town in the midst of the scrambled past and the idealized future is there to ease the shock and dispel the fears of those who are about to encounter the meaning of Southern California in its most concentrated form. The older generation may not take LSD, but when they go to Disneyland, they are taking real trips through heightened space and time. The Gothic cathedral summed up the world view of the medieval town; Disneyland is the technological cathedral of Southern California. If this sounds flippant and journalistically clever, but not really true, then the foreigner to California should visit Lincoln Savings and Loan's "Great Moments with Mr. Lincoln," or see Bell Telephone's 360-degree vision of "America the Beautiful," or get on General Electric's "Carousel of Progress," or ultimately take Monsanto's "Adventure Through Inner Space." The fantasies of the hippies, at least, are in better taste than those of the middle classes they have left behind, for it is in the small-town setting that the sanctimonious Babbitts of Lincoln Savings and Loan run a coin-operated Lincoln concession in which a mechanical effigy of President Lincoln recites a speech for those who sit in the dim religious light of the theater. To preserve the dignity of the apparition, the usherette asks, in prayerful tones, that the solemnity of the occasion be respected and that no photograph be taken. This request, no doubt, helps the Lincoln souvenir gift shop which awaits the visitor upon the completion of his patriotic trip. Ironically enough, the speech chosen by our capitalistic guardians of the past is one that warns us of the dangers of civil war.

The impact of the scrambling of history in Los Angeles was first noticed by Nathanael West in his novel, *The Day of the Locust*. His "Sargasso of the Imagination" is now Disneyland. It was Walt Disney's insight that one could make a fortune, not by making movies with a studio lot, but by charging admission. But West's artistic prophecies point up another quality of Los Angeles fantasy life: the longer one lives at this edge of history, the more his vatic nerves begin to tremble. People who come here suddenly feel like making apocalyptic prophecies. Normal intellectuals who would be quite embarrassed to do anything of the sort back east suddenly find themselves filling up with a dreadful noise. West started it all with his "Burning of Los Angeles":

He told himself that it didn't make any difference because he was an artist, not a prophet. His work would not be judged by the accuracy with which it foretold a future event but by its merit as painting. Nevertheless, he refused to give up the role of Jeremiah. He changed "pick of America's madmen" to "cream" and felt almost certain that the milk from which it had been skimmed was just as rich in violence. The Angelenos would be first, but their comrades all over the country would follow. There would be civil war.[6]

Novelist Budd Schulberg was writing an introduction for a new edition of West's work when Los Angeles went up in flames before his eyes during the Watts riot. And Thomas Pynchon has accepted the tradition

of Nathanael West to present, in the performance of
the Jacobean play that Oedipa watches, a rehearsal
of the coming American civil war:

> Oedipa found herself after five minutes sucked utterly
> into the landscape of evil Richard Wharfinger had
> fashioned for his seventeenth century audiences, so
> preapocalyptic, death-wishful, sensually fatigued, unpre-
> pared, a little poignantly, for that abyss of civil war
> that had been waiting, cold and deep, only a few years
> ahead of them.[7]

And even as urbane a writer as *The New Yorker*'s
Christopher Rand has made his own contribution to
the literature of apocalypse:

> We are already engaging in technological violence
> abroad; and the great religious teachers, not to mention
> Sigmund Freud, tell us that violence begets a mood
> leading to more violence, which in this case might mean
> more violence at home. . . . If the country gets badly
> troubled one can imagine such a schism opening up,
> perhaps over the issues of race and Manifest Destiny.
> And perhaps Dixie might join with the West in such
> a schism, as was likewise foreshadowed in '64.[8]

But the prospect is not totally bleak; or, at least,
if the worst happens, there still is the chance that after
apocalypse the millenium of "The Age of Aquarius"
will appear over the ashes of the previous order. In
the culture of the black man and the "white Negro"
one can catch a glimpse of the culture of the twenty-
first century.

The businessman mistakes the black man when he
sees in Watts only an unemployed people cut off from
the appliances of American life. Watts may be far
from white suburbia, but this distance has given it

room in which to create. Because the realization of fantasy is so integral a part of the Southern California way of life, Watts is as different from Harlem as Los Angeles is from New York. Under the permissive sun the black man is as free as the white to act out his fantasies, "don robes, and go out and change the world." The riot of 1965 called Watts into existence, for it gave to an indistinct slurb in the Los Angeles sprawl the boundary, shape, and form of a new cultural identity. Karl Marx has said that "Force is the midwife of every old society pregnant with a new one." Now that force has brought Watts into existence, the easy realization of fantasy that Los Angeles allows has given it space in which to express itself in more sublimated forms. The first anniversary of the 1965 riot was a community bonfire, which has since grown into the annual Watts festival of the arts. Now as one moves around in Watts he senses an ethos and the beginnings of what may become a real culture that the black man is creating for himself, and for us. With the Watts Happening Coffee House, with Budd Schulberg's school for writers (his own rseponse to the Watts riot), with the new proposed community arts center near the Watts Towers, one senses the possibilities of a Los Angeles that will be all the better because of the presence of the black man.

Undoubtedly, some of the new possibilities are the usual Hollywood movie-set landscape, and it is quite possible that second-generation black men, being human, are not necessarily going to do better than second-generation dust-bowlers did with their Disneylands and Knott's Berry Farms. Nevertheless, there is no reason to think that all of the experiments will fail. The revival of Swahili may seem ridiculous, but it is no more ridiculous than the revival of Irish was at the turn of the century. It seemed to many an Englishman (and Irishman as well) that Dublin had little to offer in the face of London and Paris, and the revival of Irish and Gaelic games only tended to strengthen his conviction of Irish primitiveness. But the nativistic movement that contained these clumsy gropings toward a revitalization of industrial civilization was still large enough to contain the work *in English* of Yeats, Synge, Joyce, O'Casey, and O'Connor. There is no reason to doubt, but there is much reason to hope, that what Dublin did for Great Britain, Watts could do for America. Certainly the enervated culture of white suburbia could stand the stimulation that a black nativistic movement could contribute, and if civil war or the San Andreas Fault does not ruin the chances, the black man may make Los Angeles a far greater city. But most likely, as happened before in Ireland, the cultural renaissance and the revolution will go on at once, and "there will be time to murder and create."

The Irish had a national culture of centuries' duration to sustain their resurgence, but the American black man finds himself in the place where he has neither Africa nor America. For this reason the Muslims call for the traditional promised land in a separate black nation in the South. The idea is unthinkable, but so was the dismemberment of the British Empire contained in the founding of the Irish Free State; it was force and an anarchy which made moderate, peaceful government impossible that made it thinkable. If apocalypse does not hurl us back to another Stone Age, and if we allow our fantasies of the future to impinge upon the present, then the triumph of the *Protestant Ethic and the Spirit of Capitalism* in bourgeois, national, and industrial culture will be replaced by the triumph of a new religious sensibility in a miscegenetic, Pythagorean, and planetary culture. In which case, the American black man, with his lack of a nation, is not behind us, but ahead of us. The whites, exulting in the work ethic, always saw the black man as the preindustrial past; it never occurred to them that he could be the post-industrial future. Now as we move from the industrial technology of meaningless work to the Pythagorean science of meaningful play, and Homo Ludens replaces Homo Faber, we are witnessing the creation of a new culture. For the black men who were left out of the old society, and for the whites who have dropped out, there are the roles of storied folk and leisured aristocrat in the new medieval order—an order in which the unemployed and the leisured share the common humanity that remains after one has subtracted the job from one's identity. As black revolutionary and white fascist, hippie and radical, technocrat and rugged individualist move toward apocalypse and/or the millennium, one thing remains certain: Los Angeles will remain at the edge of our history and will be thrust up to its hilt in the future of this country.

2

GOING BEYOND IT
AT BIG SUR

"Many of us are reincarnated American Indians who died at the hands of the white man and his technology. Now we have returned to be on the other side of the same event, but this time it is to be those who have what they think is power that are to be destroyed." The road to Big Sur's Esalen Institute is not always on earth, and as I listened to the young hippie hitchhikers I had picked up, I realized that some of the sharper turns of Highway One slipped over into another dimension. The winding two-lane highway rests on a meager shelf cut out or blasted out of the mountains, but, as with all violations of entropy, disorder was wearing away at its edges. Rubble, landslides, and signs from working crews showed that the road had to be worked on constantly to keep it open. I could see from the cliffs around me that this was the real edge of America, and I thought it was a beautiful way to end a country. The guide at my right was solicitous and was obviously trying to help me get my bearings in that post-historic landscape; he had responded to my casual question about the Earthquake by giving me the whole mythology of his San Francisco tribe. His girl friend, a plump, furry, frowzy-haired, and cuddly kind of female, was astonished that so square-looking a driver of a red Mustang (rented) should have heard of the California Apocalypse when the Haight-Ashbury itself had only just finished exhausting the subject. The boy was not quite so intent on appearances. At first his talk had been very Latinate, as if to show a middle-class type that he knew what he was doing in dropping out of Stanford or Berkeley, but after our conversation warmed up over the prophecies of occultist Edgar Cayce, he relaxed into a more hip language.

"Aren't you being a bit vindictive?" I asked in response to his vision.

"They are free to walk out of their fantasies and be part of the New Age, but, of course, most of them will not. They will hold on tight like misers clinging to the old money-reality, and so they will only force themselves to learn by dying—just as we did once before. For those who are free enough to let go, there will be room in the New Age, but for LBJ and the others there will be only a Stone Age life in the backwaters of an interplanetary civilization."

"And that, I take it, must be where the flying saucers make their appearance," I said laughingly, but still in an effort to pace him.

"Dig. We're the advance guard of a whole new civilization, not of action but consciousness. Like you were thinking about the Earthquake, and then you picked us up, and here we are continuing your thought."

"*Synchronicity,* huh? Just like the *I Ching?* Maybe *you* ought to go up to Esalen to give a seminar."

The girl's face popped up into the rear-view mirror. "That's great! We're headed for Esalen too. What are you going for?"

"Alan Watts on 'The Future of Consciousness,' but I think the seminar has already started here. But getting back to the flying saucers, why have they chosen you people and not demanded to be taken to our leader, LBJ?"

At that he settled back comfortably into the corner by the door and began to gather his thoughts. "Have you read any Tolkien?" he said.

"I just started him this summer, but I haven't finished the third volume yet."

"Keep going; it's the Appendix that has the heart of the thing. You see, *The Lord of the Rings* is the *real* history of this planet. The kids are really digging it because it's their story. I mean like there are a lot of karmic refugees from Atlantis around; that's what the generation gap is all about. It's not the same old gang of souls on earth any more. Anyway, Tolkien gets by the grownups as a fantasy, and even some of the kids take it in that way, but once it's inside, the unconscious takes off the fantasy wrapper and knows it's the real story. Once the Valar were here, then man attempted to attack the Lands of the Furthest West. The Valar asked the One to be released from their custodianship of the planet, Atlantis sank, and the good refugees spread all over the Earth. Tolkien calls Atlantis 'Númenor,' but it's the same thing."

"Hmmm, well, if that's the past, what's the future?"

He smiled conspiratorially and began to sing in imitation of Mick Jagger: "We are wa-ai-ting. We are wa-ai-ting for something to come out of somewhere."

"The Rolling Stones," I said, damn glad I knew the album.

"Dig. It's the return of the Valar. Dig it? We're spreading the good news right under everybody's nose. Like they used to say in Sunday school, those who have ears, let them hear. Only this time round it's to hear the Rolling Stones, the Beatles, and the Grateful Dead. That's Esalen up ahead. You can let us out at the gate; I've got a bath card to let me in. Thanks a lot for the lift; it's turned out to be a really groovy rap. You'll like Esalen; *you'll* be able to get a lot out of it."

And with that prediction, half complimentary and half condescending, he and his cuddly bear got out. I laughed inside at his farewell; evidently he felt I wasn't beyond hope, despite my red Mustang and green blazer. History had been kind to me and I was granted the privilege of still being in my twenties as the New Age was about to begin in the summer of 1967. The planetary children had arrived. As I drove down the hill into Esalen I remembered Arthur C. Clarke's science fiction novel, *Childhood's End,* which I had read over and over again in high school. Now the novel seemed partly prophetic: the children were a different species from their parents, even if the Overlords had not appeared to serve as midwives to the death of "man."

II

The condition of history that I left behind me was L.A. in preparation for the police riot at Century

City; as it turned out, it was one of the first attacks of the lower-middle class upon the white upper-middle class, and was one of the events which showed LBJ that he couldn't run for another term without bayoneted troops framing his campaign speeches. But since I had not come back to L.A. to attend demonstrations, I felt like heading out from the city for the prophetic wilderness of Big Sur. Because I had not stopped to spend the night along the way on my drive up from L.A., I arrived early for my seminar. Consequently, all the people of another seminar were already locked in their own newly discovered intimacy. There was no place for me to enter, for like a rounded sphere that was closed in upon itself, the seminar enjoyed its own circular solitude. And so I stood without and gazed in at the proceedings. From what I could tell at my distance, the seminar was richly attended by middle-aged ladies from San Mateo, for whom Alan Watts played out the role of a very continental magister. After grandiloquent remarks amid candlelight and admiring eyes, the seminar concluded with a harp concert performed by Watts's son-in-law.

The next morning I planned on doing little but waiting for the beginning of my own seminar, but the waitress told me that I could not hang around all day, drinking coffee and looking at the Pacific through the windows of the rustic dining room. And so with no space open to be intimate and joyous with anyone, I took my camera and drove up the highway to Nepenthe for lunch and Point Lobos for the afternoon.

When I returned to Esalen late that afternoon, the

old-time Esaleners were gathering and hugging one another all over the place. The ladies' club was gone and a newer and younger group was encountering one another. I walked through the hugging into the bar and found myself a quiet corner slightly to the side of the phenomenon and wondered whether I was going to have to spend three days in the corner. Then Mike Murphy, the president of Esalen, walked in. I did not recognize him immediately from his pictures, and his red alpaca sweater and black turtleneck made him appear to be someone who had stepped over from a country club golf course, but his importance became obvious as he was more luxuriantly hugged than any of the others. I still wasn't used to the Esalen style, so the Roman handshakes in which you massaged the bicep of your partner seemed foreign. There was an opening at the bar next to me, so Mike walked over and we introduced ourselves. He stood tall and smiled with extraterrestrial eyes that gazed into you. All the sudden hippie talk about the aliens moving unknown among us took on a new light; there was just something uncanny about Mike's radiant smile. He seemed too strong and innocent for a man in his mid-thirties, and there was such an unearthly and yet, paradoxically, down-to-earth manner to him that the only one I could compare him to was Michael Valentine Smith in Heinlein's *Stranger in a Strange Land.* Yet you couldn't be ill at ease with him, because he looked into you with an anticipation that was positively complimentary. I was no longer a questioned presence, but Mike's personal guest. It was impossible not to like him immediately.

I remembered reading somewhere that Mike had

spent a year and a half in meditation in the Ashram at Pondicherry, and it was this aspect and his printed comments about "the tired Eastern liberal view of man" that had attracted me to Esalen. Listening to Mike I was glad I was by the blue Pacific, with the New York intelligentsia and the black Atlantic far behind. Since Mike was talking about all the hippies who were fleeing the Haight-Ashbury to crash at Esalen, I told him about the Earthquake mythology that I had picked up from the hitchhiking couple. To embellish the apocalypse, I threw in all the other prophets of the California disaster and asked if he thought Esalen would be safe. The bartender, himself with long hair and Indian headband, poured our wine and told Mike not to worry, for that's why he had come here. It was clear that the quake that was to hit the evil cities would not destroy the unbelievably beautiful Big Sur. The minds in Esalen, in the Zen Monastery at Tassajara, and at the Catholic Hermitage at New Camaldoli would keep back the evil vibrations. The quake would strike behind Big Sur, and turn it into an island, which was an even more appropriate place to locate the lamaseries of the Aquarian Age. What Lindisfarne and Iona did for the Dark Ages of Europe, Big Sur could do for the Dark Age of America.

It was time for dinner. Since this time we were all strangers together, everyone opened up and introductions were exchanged. At dinner I found myself sitting next to a psychologist from Florida and his wife and a gynecologist, and his wife, from Livermore. This new professional group began to make Esalen seem like a holiday cruise: looking out the window at the sunset over the Pacific, I felt almost as if we were headed out for Hawaii. But over the candlelight, stoneware, and rough boards, the linen and silver of a luxury liner seemed safely distant. It was then that I had my first "sensory-awakening experience" and knew that I really was at Esalen.

It was the bread. James Baldwin, in *The Fire Next Time,* says that America will never really have soul until it stops eating the white paste it calls bread. To someone taking the American system of priorities for granted, the remark seems frivolous; but Feuerbach was closer to the truth than Betty Crocker when he said: *"Der Mensch ist was er isst."* The bread was an undecipherable blend of several grains, and when you took it with milk, it worked together like white meat of turkey and Pinot Chardonnay. Clearly, the baker, Edward Taylor, was a Zen master of a craft that becomes an art because of the religious consciousness in which it is performed. With the death of the last male Shaker, America had lost that reverence for the profound simplicity of the craft. Everything that was cheap, shoddy, and deceitfully wrapped in "country farms" packaging rose in my mind and turned in my stomach. I could see a picture of coast-to-coast food distributors serving all the restaurants the same frozen cardboard french fries, water-injected ham steaks, papier-mâché peas, and a carbonated water called beer. Orwell had good sense when he characterized 1984 as a time when good food was as unobtainable as sexual love.

After dinner we went into the seminar room for the first session. The room was as large as a classroom, but the stone fireplace, the beamed ceiling, and the windows all along one side that overlooked the sun deck dispelled any institutional atmosphere. Over the fireplace was a large psychedelic painting and several Chinese calligraphic works; in spite of the rows of folding chairs, the room was simply a converted living room. The seminar started very slowly with brief talks by Alan Watts, David Barr, an Episcopal priest and chaplain to Bishop Pike, and Paul Lee, a professor of philosophy at Santa Cruz. It was clear that Watts was still in the frame of mind of the previous seminar: the lecturer and the ladies' club. Everything was soft and easy, a scolding of American civilization for its adolescent bad taste. One long-haired, hippie-looking member of the group grew impatient and began to slap the seminar into shape by proclaiming the drug-based revolution of the young that was pulling down the curtain on the civilization of the grownups. Ira Einhorn had announced his presence and the seminar began to change. But as it moved in his direction, it simply broadened its rejection of science until an almost Amish-like purity was achieved.

Ira's politics were more developed than those of other hippies I had met before, so I was privileged to meet a Yippie a year before he surfaced into the media. Once in the center of the seminar, Ira did not hesitate to dominate the conversation by interrupting others continually, but you could see from his style that he did not do it with malice. It was just that drugs had made him autistic. His vision of history was McLuhanesque, and he spoke in a jargon that was probably what happens when you take a bright Jewish boy on his way to becoming a sociologist and startle him into another consciousness with LSD. The next solo performance came from a large, heavy, middle-aged man who spoke with a deep voice and a re-strained intensity. He spoke of the neo-cortex of the brain and evolution; he sounded like a doctor, but he was Stanley Keleman, "a practitioner of the bioener-getics approach developed initially by Dr. Alexander Lowen." With a de Chardin vision of evolution on one side and a McLuhan popeyed view of history on the other, Watts began to realize that he was not going to sleep-talk his way through this seminar, and the energy level of the group, very slowly, began to rise.

After an hour or so of an attack on science and technology, the criticism began to sound too much like a one-sided harangue, so I decided to speak in favor of technology—which was a pleasant change from my usual role at M.I.T. I reminded Watts of the engineer from the Jet Propulsion Laboratory who, at the success of one of the Mariner shots, cried for all the people in the world who could not be part of the fulfillment of man's destined journey into space. After my remark a fellow with Pancho Villa mustache began blending ethology and Vico, but people were getting tired and restless, and so we broke up, and John Bleibtreu came over and continued his discus-sion with Ira and me. John was bright and swift, and you could tell that the things he was putting together were all coming out of his own imagining. But for all his bright falconry, he still left you plenty of sky to move around in with him. Ira came on all over you like the weather in Cuernavaca: rain and sunlight at the same time. He had the plump, affectionate envelopment of a Jewish mother, but it made me slightly uneasy to realize that he was going to love everybody whether he liked it or not and that, in many ways, love was his newly discovered instrument of aggression.

Although the seminar was an intellectual one and not a group therapy encounter, the psychology to which Esalen is dedicated could not help but affect the seminar. Our group was not a twenty-four-hour marathon, yet we still found that the rate at which we were experiencing things began to accelerate. And once in the excitement of that accelaration, we all knew instinctively that it was senseless to come to Esalen and continue to operate with all our old convenient categories and distinctions. I made the mistake of thinking in terms of people's jobs: Ira was an acid head with no visible means of support, very dubious; Stanley was cagey about his occupation, so he must be some kind of chiropractor; John was the author of *The Parable of the Beast*—he was O.K. What I had failed to realize was that at Esalen we were no longer living in an industrial culture in which a man's job provided his identity. It became obvious there that if a man could not survive the subtraction of his job from his identity, then there wasn't really much to him in the first place. At Esalen the way the individual experiences is called into question in his self-encounter in the context of others encountering him. When group experience is lifted up into the form of a ritual-game, then the old habitual way one behaves is made to seem the more artificial and unreal. In this sense Esalen is a step toward another culture, a culture in which automation will force us to encounter one another no longer on economic terms: which is probably one good reason why Esalen is the exclusive preserve of the professional upper-middle class. As we throw away the industrial masks that disguise our humanity behind our productive functions, we are also forced to throw away our habitual privacy. What goes on at Esalen is invariably what goes on inside you when your nineteenth-century privacy and decorum are assaulted.

The mixed nude bathing at Esalen is, of course, the most notorious example of casting off the old privacy of industrial culture, and I had nothing against going down to the baths, but not knowing exactly where they were, I was not about to barge in by myself. The old-time Esaleners had rushed to the baths after the seminar, and so the newcomers had to gather by themselves and wonder what they were going to do with the rest of the evening. Since there was little else to do, we all went out onto the sun deck. A group of hippies was beginning to form around the fireplace to play flutes and Congo drums. As they stood around in the circle, they passed a joint among themselves. This made one couple feel very naughty, and I could see that the wife's attitude was ambiguous. The mother of a teenage daughter in her was frightened, yet the woman in her was glad that she would have something on her smart-aleck daughter when she got back to "her local community."

Her husband's nervousness, however, began to be shared by me when one teenager started circulating among the grownups with a six-inch hunting knife.

The kid was pretty freaked-out and seemed intent on proving the point that he could make these grownups reject him. If he had been really serious, he would have got what he was after, but he only played at being violent, and so we played at not rejecting him. But the kid was not the only one with a knife; all the hippies were wearing them, supposedly to help them scratch out an Indian existence in the Santa Lucia Mountains. Still, it looked more like the six-month-old movement of Love was discovering its underside of Hate. Some of the hippies looked radiantly Christ-like in their long robes and flowing hair, but most looked as if they were tagging along for a free ride. To come up close to any movement in history is to discover a coarse and grainy texture, so in looking at these love-hate hippies, you could easily conjure up the train of thieves, whores, pimps, and madmen that must have trailed behind Christ during his short three-year movement in Palestine. Anyone who had anything at all going for him in civilization was clearly not about to be in that procession. Watching one hippie smoke his joint and fondle his knife, I felt uncomfortable and was annoyed that I was uncomfortable. But the sea air was enough to calm your nerves, and I forced myself to relax and accept the presence of Big Sur under all that surface noise.

After breakfast the next morning, Mike Murphy herded us off, like children at a summer camp, to the swimming pool to do Tai Chi with Gia-fu, the resident instructor of this Chinese meditational ballet. The day before I had seen some people making fools out of themselves through strange motions awkwardly performed. Now I discovered it was my turn to look silly, but since there was little purpose in coming to Esalen and not being willing to make a fool of yourself, I was prepared to go along with the organized activity. In his bright orange sweater which stood out against the gray overcast day, Gia-fu began to teach us the technique. He explained how the mind could only be quieted and made to rest in the Other if the body were calmed. He lifted one leg and put his long slender fingers together in the attitude of a rooster. Across from me a dyed-blond thirty-nine-year-old divorcee stared out at us in terror and embarrassment, and her eyes began to look like two independently caged animals. Try as she might, she simply could not stand at rest on one foot: the dissonance in her eyes was clearly in evidence in her body. Gia-fu's first lesson proved itself. Looking at the woman, you could sense that inside her body it must have felt something like twenty cigarettes and a dozen cups of coffee in an hour. But Gia-fu was kind and we were all clumsy enough that she did not have to feel too bad.

After about ten minutes the dancelike quality of the exercises began to take me over. With the help of the morning sea air and the mountain atmosphere, I began to feel really good. Body information began to come in from parts inside my muscles and tissues that I didn't know existed. This was my second sensory-awakening experience. I could sense physical tones and could tell how an old nerve anastomosis from an operation really made one arm different from another. The tissue itself in my limbs seemed to produce a new sentience, and I grew to resent the affront of my impaired arm. My body felt new in the way it had four months after I had quit smoking and no longer awoke drugged and sluggish in the morning. I could tell that if I made a habit out of these exercises I would know just where body and mind touched one another. After twenty minutes I could see how worthwhile it was to make a fool out of yourself now and then.

I couldn't have returned to the seminar in better spirits. Like some Pentecostal Holy Roller touched by a tongue of flame, I suddenly found myself speaking better than ever before. Paul Lee christened me "word freak," as people laughed, marveled, and broke into applause. No longer the outsider kicked out of the dining room by the waitress, I began to feel like an honor student receiving praise and encouragement from the teachers. As other people in the group found themselves beginning to expand, the seminar was transformed into a play in which we were all actors. Lines of opposition began to appear between members in different parts of the group and I found myself engaged in an agon with Ira. Watts responded to this sudden stumbling into form and switched roles from soloist to conductor.

While directors all over the world were straining to find a drama beyond mimesis, we had all crossed over from unstructured reality into something that was half drama, half ritual-game, and yet it was a lived performance and not an observed imitation of reality. But best of all, we were free of the anti-authoritarian hatred that possesses avant-garde drama. When you walk into a small theater, you are attacked by the actors: they are free, you are sup-

posed to be in chains; they scream at you to stand up
and be counted, yet you know that if you walked up
to the stage, writing your own dialogue as you went,
the burgher behind the actor's mask would follow the
script, or get rid of you if you proved to be a nui-
sance. For, after all, people were paying good money
to be so abused. Why should we go to the theater
to be abused by arrogant beings who interrupt the
light and demand that we remain immobile in their
artificially created darkness? Why should we pay to
see nakedness in darkness when we can be naked in
sunlight?

As we all fell into place at Esalen, I saw how happenings, love-ins, guerrilla theater, and drama itself
were simply rehearsals for the ultimate performance,
the next step in human cultural evolution. We had
come to Esalen from all over the country, and now,
like coins tossed for the *I Ching,* we created a geom-
etry larger than ourselves. The uncanny feeling of the
group as a single psychic organism composed of each
of us grew with each day until rumors of the phenomenon brought in observers, who, by their very
presence, destroyed the phenomenon itself.

The talk in the sessions so stimulated everyone
that it spilled over into the bar, the sun deck, the
hillsides, and the baths. I had not yet gone down to
the baths, so I was ready to stroll down there with
the others to continue our discussion in a rather
Greek atmosphere. With John Bleibtreu and Stanley
Keleman, I went down for a before-dinner soak. The
baths are a simple cinder-block structure that hangs
about fifty feet above the rocks of the Pacific. Behind
it are the steeper cliffs, and, farther up, Highway

One. Removed some distance from the main buildings, the baths sit in a space all their own like a shrine. My first impression settled mainly on the sulphur smell of the hot springs, the cinder-block texture, and the general locker-room ethos, an ethos I have always disliked because of its homosexual, fanny-slapping, athletic camaraderie. But I pushed my first impressions aside and we all plunked ourselves in like tea bags and began to steep in the communal broth. Ira was there, and so our agon about visions—natural head vs. acid head—began all over again. It was becoming a drag, but John and Stanley helped keep it going, and then two girls came in from the other side, and that helped matters quite a bit.

Ostensibly the baths are split into halves for the sexes, with dark midnight kept for mixing, but the braver and more beautiful bodies were willing to be seen in sunlight, so there were times when people crossed over. As the girls came in to join us in our large tub, I could feel the atmosphere being refreshed at once. The male, locker-room ethos was expelled by the overwhelming power of a naked female body. The two girls were both quite attractive: one was a dark brunette of about thirty, the other a young blonde of about twenty who had come down to Esalen with Ira from the Monterey Pop Festival. Diana, the young blonde, was quite nervous and embarrassed. The adventure was clearly not her idea. She really had nothing to be embarrassed about, for she had a beautifully voluptuous body. As I tried, as discreetly as possible, to admire her young and perfect breasts, I thought of William Carlos Williams' poem, "The Pink Church":

—above and beyond
  your teaching stands
the Pink Church:
          the nipples of
a woman who never
    bore a
      child . . .

and of how much I preferred thinking of poetry in Big Sur than in the British Museum. And so we sat, the six of us, in the afternoon sun obeying the canonical hours in a post-Christian hermitage devoted to the resurrection of the body. The steam made every muscle in me melt, and I unthought myself sensuously into the orange afternoon light.

And on we talked until it was time to go up for California wine and Esalen bread. As I got up slowly from the tank, I was surprised to see just how slowly I did get up. The baths had put my metabolism into slow motion. I felt as loose as the living water from which I had just emerged, like some newly evolving life struggling onto an alien beach. As I slowly dragged my sensory-awakened body up the hill with John, I watched the brunette collapse in delight from the utter exhaustion brought on by the baths. She lay in the tall grass with an archaic smile upon her lips, so John bent down to kiss her, which was the only decent thing to do under the circumstances, but I struggled on like some Spenserian knight wandering in the Bower of Bliss.

In the evening more and more hippies began to appear around the hillsides. The Haight-Ashbury had been taken over by newsmen, filmmakers, and teeny-boppers from the Midwest, so now the gentle people were leaving the city behind to the plastic hippies of CBS. As I overheard one of them say to his brother: "We've got to get the people out of the cities; they're full of bad vibrations. It's fucking up even good heads. We've got to split and make our thing in the country." Here again was the ageless mythic pattern of the attack on the cities. Within the city a man could see no farther than the battlements and walls, but outside in the desert, the stars weighed one down in a pastoral vision that remembered Noah and the Flood and the original covenant with God.

The persistence of myth is irresistible, and though we have changed the content of history, we seem never to have altered its mythic structure. Inside the city was a celebration of power, whether it was the Ur of Abraham, the Egypt of Moses, the Israel of Amos, the Mandarin cities of Mao, or the New York of Normans Mailer and Podhoretz. Now the liberal technocratic state of California had become another Egypt, and another tribe was heading out for manna in the wilderness brought down by flying saucers. The story which I was told by the hippie I had picked up on my way up to Big Sur became the theme for the cover of that week's San Francisco *Oracle*. An American Indian face filled the vibrating ether of space over three mountains inscribed as San Francisco. Just taking off, or, perhaps, just landing, were three flying saucers. The syncretic imagination of the hippies was, and is, planetary in its inclusiveness, for Japanese Zen, Indian Yoga, Atlantean legends, Navaho myths, Plains Indian visions, fundamentalist sects, UFO's, and modern chemistry were all rolled into one joint. If the young of Jean-Luc Godard's Paris were the children of Marx and Coca-Cola, these were the children of McLuhan and Du Pont living in a retribalized Global Village and achieving "better things for better living through chemistry." To encounter such an apocalyptic vision might be expected among the messianic cargo cults of Melanesia, but to find it in the dropout children of the California affluent upper-middle class, the most highly educated generation in history, was a blow to the liberal middle-class vision of progress. The liberals had built the huge University of California and brought to the state the greatest public educational system in the history of mankind, and now, in a flash, it was all going up in smoke from the burning leaves of grass.

The tribes were not to gather in Big Sur without a ceremony of drums. The bonfires were lit, the meth had already been sniffed, and the drumming began. The fog softened the background sound of the tide and muffled the faint echo of the drums that came from the hills behind us. As the fire blazed and the drumming quickened, a boy took off his shirt and began to move his naked chest closer to the fire. Yesterday I had watched him nervously twitching; one moment his face would curl up in an involuntary snarl, and the next moment he would affirm his surroundings in an expansive love-smile. Now he looked as if he had sped himself up with enough methedrine for an enormous crash. He glanced around the fire as if he were menaced by some unknown, but then came back to his fascination with the fire. Very quietly he began to chant to himself, as he rose to lean his chest out over the flames,

"Blood, Blood, Blood, Hate, Hate, Hate." His chant grew louder so that one of the more Christlike of the drummers opened his eyes to gaze with concern at the freaked-out kid. His hair was very short, and it was clear from his looks that he had not been with the movement very long. Zen and the *I Ching* meant nothing to him, but the weeks of grass, speed, and acid seemed to be taking him into a hell that increased his contempt and resentment for the hippies who surrounded him with talk of love. Love seemed to be something this kid had never known, but what he did know about life he now was prepared to chant in the faces of all the hate-repressed flower children. I was very simply afraid and ashamed that I was afraid. It was one thing to celebrate, following R. D. Laing, the schizophrenic as the culture hero of an alienated society, and it was quite another thing to stare unperturbed into the violent eyes of a person who has gone out of his mind. Ira said that once you have gone out of your own mind you know how to handle other people who go out there too, but the direction in which this bare-chested fire worshiper was moving was not the same one that attracted me. I had had enough of the whole conjuration, but I knew that in leaving I was only proving the broader humanity that Ira practiced beyond my limitations. I could not attend on freaks with loving care. The underside of Esalen was exposed and I felt uneasy, sensing that it was I who was really being exposed.

I had come to Esalen supposedly to find something outside the industrial culture of the great American middle class, but when confronted by the sexuality and madness that lay beyond my old borders, I rushed back. I was threatened because I knew I could not pass the test, and so, for all my cherished natural-head experiences, my agon with Ira was not valid. I had no right to attack his way unless I could walk through this hell without any beast within me rising in recognition of the beasts around me. For all my expensively acquired knowledge, I had no knowledge that was of any use in this world. I had spent ten years in and out of fellowships, continents, degrees, and academic publications, but I was still no higher up than I was at eighteen, before that grand tour had begun. I had been traveling sideways into many interesting places, but I had not moved one inch up. I could put down the sillier pretensions of the hip-pies and dazzle some people by pointing in the right direction, but I had not gone there and come back. It was all disembodied knowledge that didn't yet belong to me. I knew what I said was right, but I also knew that it was getting time to shut up and take a different kind of grand tour in the next decade. And so I went to bed on the third night full of a self-disgust I had not expected to find in Esalen's world of "More Joy."

The discussion at the next morning's session was on the role of drugs in the future of consciousness, and here the seminar's very shortsighted vision of the future became obvious. The future talked about was nothing more than the present, 1967, the summer of the hippie. It was not about the emerging civil war between the opposite ends of the great American middle class, it was not about the ecological disasters of our technology, it was not about the world-wide famine of 1975, or the doubling of the earth's population by 2000; it was about acid, pure and simple. This was Ira's element, and so he declaimed: "Within a few years America will undergo a complete transformation of its consciousness, as every thirteen-year-old turns on and walks out of his father's tract home, as Buddha walked out of his father's palace." The revolution to end all revolutions was at hand. If the previous night had left me confused, the sunlight of the morning gave me enough of a mood to make one last response to Ira's preaching. I agreed with him that LSD was a political tool, or weapon, but I wanted to draw a distinction between mysticism and the forceful embodiment of visions in millenarian crusades where the visions are organized by those who don't have them. The natural apertures for light were the eyes, and for those whose eyes had been closed by America, it was, perhaps, necessary to crack open their skulls with acid to let in a little light; but even that light should be sufficient to see that the way to self-mastery was not through jamming in a penny behind the fuse which turned on the lights but burned out the wires for good.

The straight people beamed and expressed their approval of me and made me their champion; they could live with my way, for my shabby-genteel pride in my own self-made visions and ideas did not threaten their own successful lives as much as Ira's vision did. But my pride struck a responsive chord in the other proud man of the seminar, and Watts moved in to the defense of drugs by pointing out that if one turned down acid because it was cheap and easy like a penny, it was often merely because of a spiritual pride that wished to congratulate itself on having arrived at a place through an unnecessarily long and hard way. Ira felt my academic purism was the old hierarchical hang-up, a resentment of the fact that LSD had democratized the mystic vision. I responded by saying that the industrial mysticism of Leary was no more satisfying than the industrial sexuality of Hugh Hefner, but I knew the agon was futile. I was the old nineteenth-century self fighting to save its privacy in an age when solitude was regarded as a failure to take the next step in human cultural evolution.

What did it matter if the hippies were the mirror images of Detroit engineers? LSD industrialized mysticism, but it also subverted industrial materialism. My private vision would never shake history up, so these mass-produced media-mystics would keep history moving by kicking it along; and if evil appeared in the process, well, evil was the way in which the historical process worked. We were all caught in a shoddily built house in which the lights had gone out. The hippies wanted the penny jammed behind the fuse, the radicals wanted to burn the house down and make for the exits by the light of the flames, and the moderates wanted to call in the "experts" who had built the house in the first place. And as for me, I simply depended on some personal insight to help me see my way out of the social dark. Obsessed by the image of the darkened house, I allowed myself to slip into a fantasy in which I was walking around in it. I couldn't recognize the place and felt lost as I moved about in the dark, half-formed structure. As I wandered around, people would stop me and very lucidly explain the situation. One was very calm and said that the directors had a great machine that would take care of everything. Another was organizing a march to confront the machine. The last one simply laughed and said: "We're going to burn it down, baby." And as I looked into each one's eyes, I realized that they were all insane, that, in fact, I was wandering around in an insane asylum.

There are only two choices open to those who have discovered that society is a madhouse. In the tradition of Plato's cave, they can withdraw and seek light elsewhere to discover the larger landscape in which the madhouse is located. Or, if that Platonic tradition of the Good seems merely an infantile fantasy, they can deny self-determination to the insane majority and burn the madhouse to the ground to force people out into the open. Looking at the Platonic and Marxist choices, I knew I would withdraw.

I had come to Esalen to find a charismatic institution that was free of the routines that had entangled the university, but I had found only another human institution, full of flaws and contradictions, even if they were greatly different from M.I.T.'s. If I was seeking to gain a perspective on history by getting out of history, I still had further to go. Since "The Future of Consciousness" had not taken me very far ahead, I decided to step to the side and look back at the religious past. The hippie who had hitchhiked with me had told me that there was a monastery nearby where one could stay as a guest in a hermit's cell. Since I was tired of Ira's aggressive love and its negating embrace, and since I disliked the competitiveness that Ira and Watts brought out in me, I decided to withdraw to my natural nineteenth-century solitude and spend the afternoon at the monastery, if only to hear the chanting of vespers.

Driving south along Highway One for about eight miles, I came to the sign for the monastery: The Hermitage of New Camaldoli. I expected to find the gate just off the highway, but found only a dirt road going up the mountainside. The idea of tooling up the mountainside in my rented red Mustang did not appeal to me, so I decided to park the car off the road and walk up. The more I thought about the walk, the more I liked the idea, but the road proved much longer than I thought. It was really a broad mountain trail full of switchbacks that gave you no indication of whether or not the next one was the last, and I began to realize that the monastery must be at the very top of the coastline, some fourteen hundred feet above the sea. But the rewards of the climb were not so far away, for after a short walk I found myself up above the clouds in the sunlight once again.

It had been foggy and overcast at Esalen for days, and I had had no sense of how just a few hundred feet above us there was sunlight everywhere. Now I could look out over the sea, which was covered with a cotton blanket of clouds to the edge of the horizon, but at the shore there were patches of blue where the lower peaks and cliffs jutted out in the sunlight. The rocks and the few tilting trees hanging over the clouds seemed to be from the world of Japanese painting; it was easy to see why the Zen Monastery at Tassajara belonged in Big Sur. Big Sur was Western Asia: the Japanese had defeated us with their

ideology, as we had conquered them with our economics; now we had Zen and they had transistors.
This was the logical end of the American frontier,
and while we were busy conquering Asia with our
bodies, it was winning in our minds. Small wonder
that the Sierra Club and the people of Big Sur had
fought to keep the developers out. This was simply
one of the most beautiful places in the world; it had
a quality that set it apart from a merely "pretty"
landscape. Vibrations are what the hippies would
say it had, and they would be right. In the fables of
St. Brendan the Navigator, his men once set ashore
on what proved to be the back of a huge whale. But
like so many Irish legends, the tale describes another dimension of reality: the fact that there are
moments when we suddenly realize that what we
thought was the insentient rock of earth turns out
to be the back of a leviathan swimming in oceans
of space and time.

Above the fog the sun was shining hotly, so I
slowed my pace, but after a few turns of the road, I
caught a glimpse of the gate of the monastery hanging down from the top of the mountain. I rested for
a moment to prepare myself for the last little bit
of my climb and looked up at the gate, which seemed
to hang down almost within arm's reach. But when
I started up again and rounded the corner of the
switchback, I discovered that the gate wasn't just
ahead and that there were still at least half a dozen
switchbacks left. And then I laughed out loud as
my whole agon with Ira fell into the form of the
landscape. Ira had looked at LSD and the kids and
proclaimed the New Planetary Civilization of Con-

sciousness in 1967; he had forgotten that there are turns in the road of history, and at the moments when we are at a turning point, we are permitted to look out across all the curves of the road to see the end hanging down almost within our grasp; but when we come to the top of the first incline, we find that the road cuts back and we can only see what is straight in front of us, and that doesn't even seem to be going in the right direction. Standing there, I knew it was for that moment that I had turned away from Boston and Europe to come home to California. Ira's millennium and my apocalypse both fell into place.

As I reached the bend in the road, I stopped for a moment at the point which enabled me to look back in the past where I had gazed up at the monastery gate, and to the switchback which seemed to lead in the opposite direction. Slowly I turned the corner into the road and felt no longer in the mood for meditations on the tragic nature of history.

As I returned to Esalen after attending vespers at the monastery, I could see the musicians arriving for the next day's folk festival. Again the exciting and dissonant air of Esalen was stimulating beyond the serene purity of the monastery, and yet I felt a wish to nurture my contemplative quiet for a little longer. I went into the bar for a glass of wine, but the dinner lines were already forming; it was time to return completely. Greeted by my fellow members of the encounter group as a long-lost returning son, I gave in and joined that strange sense of community we had created. Once again the room was filled with the warm colors of sunset over the ocean, and as the candles were being lit on the tables, I could see that this was no time or place for anything but good food and talk. The musicians and their followers had brought a whole new sense of excitement to the place. I had had no idea that the seminar I came up for was to be followed by a festival with Joan Baez *and* Judy Collins *and* Simon and Garfunkel *and* the Chambers Brothers. Now I was really glad I had not stayed in a hermit's cell on a mountaintop.

The seminar was nearing its climax. Amid the throngs of strangers we recognized ourselves as members of an elite. We treasured the communal psyche of what had become our encounter group with the ardor of a combat team that had grown into a single mind and body under the pressure of months of fighting. Mike Murphy was clearly pleased with the things that could take place at Esalen and was going around bragging to the newcomers about our seminar. Inevitably he had to prove to the outsiders that he was not exaggerating; but in inviting them in to observe the phenomenon, Mike had forgotten that with people, as with the elementary particles of quantum mechanics, the observer interacts with the system and changes it. Joan Baez and Ralph Gleason, the music critic for the San Francisco *Chronicle,* were invited in, and for the occasion we were permitted to inaugurate a new seminar room that had just been finished.

As I walked into the candlelit and incensed room, I saw Mike on the floor in the Yoga corpse posture. I wondered what rays and vibrations he was summoning into the room, but not being a magus, I could not tell. As we assembled in the room, Watts had us join hands to perform a ritual chanting of the mantra, *"Om Ram Sri Ram Ji Ji Ram."* Watts seemed in a mood for reminiscence, and he told us how he had felt about leaving England and coming, always pushing farther west, to California in the hope of finding what we had experienced this week. The group was in such a soft and reverent mood that silence seemed to question our presence, so one of the members, the psychologist from OOE in Washington, proposed that if each told why he had come to Esalen, we woud find a single plot joining all the characters into the drama.

Watts's reminiscent mood set my own memory to working and I talked about an epiphany in Dublin's National Library while I was reading George Russell's mystical vision of revolution, *The Interpreters.* I felt then, as I read Russell and remembered Arthur C. Clarke's *Childhood's End,* that the book I was writing could not be written by anyone else, that every other available writer on Irish literature and politics would dismiss Russell's ideas and miss the profound theory of social conflict that was implicit in the vision. That sense of being drawn toward a place and discovering something of self and history in that place was the uncanny sense I had of Esalen now. Our seminar seemed like Russell's vision of revolution: a collusion of conflicting opposites in a deadly game moving toward a single overwhelming event.

My remarks had been too dramatic, and now the silence intimidated anyone from breaking it—that is, to continue the religious-testimonial mood we all were in. The encounter group ethos had allowed us to accept such uncustomary behavior as normal, but not so for the observers, and it was then that they made their presence felt. Gleason said that he had never felt so unreal in all his life as when he had come into the room, and then he went off into a long remark on the reality of the kids and their new culture which really pointed up how unreal we were. "The kids" appeared so often in this fifty-year-old critic's comments that it was obvious that he needed them just as much as suburban liberals needed ghetto blacks, so I was delighted to switch out of my reminiscent mood to have an argument with another loud-mouthed American Irishman.

Then Joan Baez stood up, looking tall, lean, and dangerous in her black leather vest and pants; all she needed to match the violence in her eyes was a riding crop with a thirty-caliber machine-gun bullet struck on the end. She said that she had never heard so much bullshit in her whole life, that there was only one question now, and that was: Which side of the war machine are you on? You're either with the kids, or against them and for the Pentagon.

Gleason's attack had been tame and good-spirited compared to the savage indignation of Joan Baez in her fury. The dimensions of the room visibly altered and light warped as it passed anywhere near her. You were attracted and repelled by her at the same time; the beautiful woman lured you on, while the mythic being clawed at your guts. She reminded me of someone, and then I remembered and answered her: she was another Maud Gonne screaming at Yeats to stop writing poems and start shooting Englishmen, or, at least, write the kind of poems that would inspire some *real men* to do the shooting; she yelled for peace with the voice of a recruiting sergeant and was forgetting that the biggest lecher was the celibate always not-thinking of sex, the biggest criminal was the chief of police, and the most violent person was the pacifist who screamed for peace with impassioned eyes that were *prima facie* evidence against himself.

It worked. The dimensions of the room returned to normal and light bounced off what was once again the body of a beautiful woman, She stood silent for a moment, stared at me as I took in the breath the long blast had cost, thought of something, and then changed her mind. The creature had decided not to destroy me; it was over. And because it was all over, she grew impatient with her surroundings and said she had to leave because the musicians at the rehearsal had not wanted her to come in the first place. But as she turned to go, one of the members of the seminar asked her very unctuously for a song. I forget the particular song she chose, but I remember how she allowed her hostility to return to this sublimated form and belted the whole thing out with proud contempt.

As we walked out, I said to Watts, *"Tetelestai.* It's over; Joan Baez was the climax of the seminar. If we continue tomorrow morning, we'll only experience the anticlimax." Watts was surprised, but tended to agree. Mike was surprised at Joan Baez's anger and felt guilty for having brought her in. I told him I thought it was appropriate for the climax. We had all escaped history and inhaled a new air outside of time; now it was time to return to history to exhale eternity in the world of action. Joan was simply the Great Goddess summoning us back with a slap. It was ritual: the slap at birth or the bishop's slap at confirmation. Joan's demeanor was frightful but the Great Goddess had several faces: she was huge and called us from her womb, she was beautiful and called us to her bed, and she was ugly and called us to death. We had all been silly boys in the encounter group; we had not known that the group psyche had already been created; when we sought to fondle it, we lost it.

But from another point of view Joan Baez had really joined in our living play with all the magnificent contradictions of her own character. Had we not played our roles, she could not have fallen into hers with the energy that proved she was a brilliant actress in the role. Part of her was the beautiful smiling girl with the sad voice that sang of all the tragedies of history; part of her was the shrill crone calling the young men to satisfy her deadly passion in "non-violent" wars. Previously in 1965 I had sat in Dublin's Abbey Theatre watching *Kathleen ní Houlihan* and had remembered how the beautiful Maud Gonne had played the old woman asking the young men to give up their marriage beds to chase the strangers from her house and "die" with her into immortality. Now in my own life and in my own country history was becoming possessed once again by the timeless mythic pattern.

I knew the seminar was drawing to a close, and I knew that those who hold onto things beyond their natural, blossoming finish find only bitterness and dried leaves in their tightening grasp. I was happy with the supportive culture of Big Sur, but for all the talk and touching, all I wanted to do was dance. The musicians were rehearsing, but a group of us stood around Joan muddling what was finished. No real dancing was possible there. After a while the room was closed up in preparation for the next day's festival. Since it was midnight, it was again time for the ritual of the baths.

There was no moon and little phosphorus in the waves that night but still the baths were better by night than by day. Candlelight and incense made up for the lack of moon, and the soft, shadowed atmosphere more than dispelled the locker-room quality of the bare cinder blocks. As I settled back to relax by soaking and listening to the surf, Diana came in and joined me in the large tub. It was interesting to see how quickly she had lost her sense of embarrassment. Before she had held onto her towel and looked supremely uncomfortable; now she was more relaxed and at ease with her voluptuous body. The sound of the surf, the dim light, and all the talking of the seminar before made us listen in silence.

Then Watts, his wife and daughter, and a hippie with an Indian peace pipe came in. I pulled in my stretched-out legs to make room for the coming immersion. The pipe was passed, and Watts exhaled his praise: "Ah, beneficent herb!" Gazing at the portly guru, I considered his U accent, his perfected taste for fine food, wines, women, and drugs, and wondered how the elderly lecherous Yeats would have struck me at touching range. To be sure, Watts made no pretenses about genius; he only claimed his rightful talent as a brilliant entertainer of the intellect

in a world of academic bores who contributed significantly to his success. The erotic and sensuous
mysticism of Watts's way of life was attractive, and
he himself was certainly an enormously likable person, but my pride told me that I did not want to
grow up to be another Alan Watts, so "I bore my
chalice safely through a throng of foes." He was a
soul resting with the devas, an elderly and wealthy
Brahman who should now be a *sanyasin,* but was
putting off the battle with his karma for another life.
Watts had enough knowledge to know what was on
top of the mountain, and he knew the road he
should take, but given the immensity of eternity, he
was in no hurry to push off in a vulgar rush.

Time passed in the penetrating heat of the baths.
When finally I rose to dress, I discovered again that
the hot springs had put my body into slow motion.
As I moved out to the railing at the cliff's edge, I
stopped. A towel seemed a harsh way to dry, so I
stood in the sea wind and let the air dry me off.
Every pore came alive as individually each tingled
and dried in a random succession all over my body.
The change from the springs to the sea wind was a
rebirth, a rediscovery of the sheer sensory quality
of being alive in a body. I could see why in the old
creation myths the primordial sea was female and
the sky was masculine: the baths assuaged you like
an amniotic fluid, but the wind astonished every
nerve to consciousness. My skin became an independent animal, and the sexuality locked in the
crotch grew along the tendrils of my nerves.

The next morning all was new in the excitement
of the festival. The dining room at breakfast was

filled with the high spirits of a kindergarten on the last day before Christmas vacation. John Bleibtreu was in an expansive mood and overintroduced me to Fritz Perls, Esalen's aged resident magister of gestalt therapy. Perls, encased in his terry-cloth jumpsuit, cast a slow turtle look at me, and then returned to the task at hand, which was giving some unsupportive therapy to one of the women in the seminar. He rose slowly and moved to another table like a turtle moving to another rock. Mike Murphy came in and sat down, and together we began to wonder how the seminar would end. I didn't want to go to the morning's session; it seemed beside the point of last night, which I wanted to keep as sharp as possible, but when the other members came to call us in, there was no polite way of refusing.

It had ended for me, but it had not ended yet for the others. For days hostility had been building up in the group of twenty or so who had never spoken. They had come to Esalen for the unusual, but with so many intellectuals present from all over the country, they had been stunned into silence. All the terms, concepts, and names we slung around buzzed over them like B-52's. Now they wanted to get out from under; it was their turn. They wanted to touch and speak free of English. They chanted, sang, shouted obscenities, and performed an avant-garde oratorio above, beneath, and to the side of English. The last session ended in a combination of glossolalia and the "Silences" of John Cage.

As we returned to the main building, the crowds were beginning to arrive for the festival. Now mingling among the hippies were the very solid, Stanford-looking folk-song lovers. There was a joyous atmosphere, and all the members of the seminar strolled in the sunshine, and, for some, in the acid of their concluding trips. We greeted one another as if we had been friends for years and were hospitable to the strangers who had just come to *our* Esalen. I put away all thought of the civil war I had discussed, and settled back to enjoy the California of sunshine and guitars.

Joan Baez led the procession of musicians to the stage that had been set up on the deck of the cliffside pool. She sang a spiritual, and that set the tone for the concert. It was all the civil rights folk-song movement of the fifties and early sixties: back in those long-gone days before the expulsion of the whites from SNCC. It was beautiful and antique, and the comely audience loved it. The hippies, however, were not enthusiastic. Anytime a song resembled anything you could dance to, they would hit the sun deck to do their thing. It was plain that they were waiting for the Chambers Brothers. And so was I, but it proved to be a long wait. Another civil rights singer, with streaks of the folksy comedian, came onto the stage. He must have been loved for his politics, for he was a mediocre singer and a corny comedian.

The afternoon began to stretch out, and the Chambers Brothers seemed even further off. Finally, Simon and Garfunkel appeared and brought peace to the restless crowd of hippies with a beautiful version of *"In Nomine Domini."* They did not sermonize, and that helped. Joan Baez returned and sang more spirituals and civil rights songs, and, with her comments, brought back the New Left Revival Hour tone. Many now began to mumble openly about her pushing it a bit much. Judy Collins and Joan Baez joined in a song, and then Collins sang by herself. There was a solitude to her voice that seemed to come from the calm of a person exhausted by suffering. If Joan sang "Tear Down the Walls," you would expect to see eager men spring up to tear them down, but Judy's voice seemed somewhere beyond pathos and exhortation in the places of the soul reserved for tragedy where no Boy Scout would wish to run in to cheer her up. We were quiet; the sun was lower; we exhaled our silences and looked over to the black men to deliver us, for it was time.

Since "soul" has become a *Time* cover special, it is easy to discount the reality of the mystique; but if there ever was evidence of human beings standing ontologically above the frail attempts to lift the spirit, it was with this group. The lead singer came to the mike, knowing we had been waiting for two hours, and intoned:

BROTHER: Are you ready?
CROWD: (*weakly*) Yeah!
BROTHER: (*in a preacher's harangue*) When I ask you, "Are you ready?" I want to hear YEY-AWW like you all know where it's at. ARE YOU READY?
CROWD: YEY-AWW!
BROTHER: (*impatient with the children*) One more time. ARE YOU READY?
CROWD: (*finally with soul*) YEY-AWW!
BROTHER: Then, turn it on, brothers.

At that the transformers took over and the place went into apotheosis. I ran to the sun deck for the

dance I had been waiting for. The first girl was a
New Yorker with granny-goose lenses, bored counte-
nance, and spastic movements that looked more like
St. Vitus's dance than a body swayed to music. Poor,
tired, transplanted New Yorker, she was used to the
black magic of the Velvet Underground and couldn't
tell Walpurgisnacht from the rites of spring. I soon
found another girl for the next number and then
began my own ascension.

I danced into a group formation with the hippies,
and then we all began a round dance about a beautiful blonde pregnant girl. She was the mirror opposite
of the New Yorker: blonde, radiant, smiling, and
a glorious dancer, as she had to be, or else her dance
of pregnancy would have been ridiculous. But she
took all those customs and dismissed them; it was
her right to feel as primordial as a dance, and she
was not going to let any recent conventions take it
away from her. With her Anatolian navel as our
ritual center, with the sunlight, the sea air, the mountains all around us, the incense and grass, the bangled
feet, the tambourines, the music, the bells and flowers, the unbrassiered women and the shirtless sun-
tanned men, I was as high as the air over it all.

There at the edge of the Pacific you could feel
the future blowing into your face and see all the new
cultures streaming behind into the wake of history,
where they would come to rest in the museums of
New York and Europe. Here you could not work
or reach out to hold them as they swept past; you
could only dance, and play, and take your fill. Later
in the winters and darkness of the East there would
be time for work. The music reached its peak, then

cut out. All of us kept up the beat in our heads and stamped it out on the wooden deck with our feet, and when the music returned, sixty feet hit the deck in a single beat. We all smiled in perfect recognition of ourselves; we were showing to the aged veterans of lunch counters what the new political consensus looked like.

The music paused and then started up in a slow ballad, and my puffing body caught up with me and asked for a drink. Gazing out over the land around me, I leaned against the wall and thought: "At twenty-nine in the summer of 1967 I danced in the twenty-first century, and in the dark remaining years ahead I will remember this free-for-all of Pacific sound and light. The days in Big Sur will last longer than the years in Cambridge. California is my home, even if I must live away from it." In high school in L.A. I had projected myself out of the lower class in dreams of J. Press suits, regimental ties, and Ivy League doctoral robes; now all that seemed "old clothes upon a stick to scare a bird." With all my T group emotions bursting out of form, I ran to exhaust them into form, and danced until there was nothing left. Then began the good-byes, the strange karmic partings, as if we knew that something else was about to begin, that *this* was over. And then, like souls departing for their birth, we left.

*Thanks be to God, I did not find
myself in a condition which obliged
me to make a merchandise of science
for the improvement of my fortune.*
RENÉ DESCARTES

3

GETTING BACK
TO THINGS AT M.I.T.

"I doubt if there is any such thing as an 'urban crisis,'
but if there were, M.I.T. could lick it in the same
way we handled the Second World War." Thus did
Professor Gordon Brown, the Dean of the School
of Electrical Engineering, peevishly reveal his suspicion of the whole purpose of the Institute's 1967
symposium on urban affairs. John Collins, then
Mayor of Boston, challenged Professor Brown and
remarked: "If we haven't learned anything this summer from Newark and Detroit, I just don't know
what will finally convince us." But Professor Brown's
theme of the forties was picked up and repeated so
often that it began to seem that the whole purpose
in calling the special symposium was to declare war
on the urban poor. From the point of view of the
poor that might have been more honest, but it certainly was not what Jerome Wiesner, the Provost
and former Scientific Adviser to President Kennedy,
had in mind when he organized the event.

No doubt Professor Brown knew what it really
was all about and expressed his disapproval of the

direction the new liberals were taking. Conservatives like Brown obviously felt that the Institute's business was with the computers and transistors that had made M.I.T. great in his time, but the liberals like Wiesner were hoping to lead the Institute beyond hardware into the design and implementation of whole new management systems for the government of a "Technological Society." Just as once before M.I.T. had displaced classical science in favor of engineering, so now it seemed about to displace engineering in favor of the behavioral sciences. As another great M.I.T. warrior of the forties, Professor George Valley, has said: "In the past, we have been grooming the student to run U.S. Steel. Now we are grooming him to run the U.S."

As a high school student in Los Angeles, I had always thought of M.I.T. as the Cal Tech of the East that had Harvard as its neighbor, but when I came back to Cambridge from California, it became clear that the Institute, in more ways than one, was the home not of Nobel physicists like Richard Feynman but of millionaire economists like Paul Samuelson. What distinguished M.I.T. from any other university was not its science but its overwhelming lust for power. I should have guessed earlier from the buildings, because M.I.T. generously gives itself away in its style of architecture. The conscious monumentality of Great Court, the fortress shape of the political science building, the Persepolis staircase of the Student Center, and the colossus of the Earth Sciences Building, all declare the power of an institution that can locally transform the economy of Massachusetts, nationally contribute to the military and economic supremacy of the United States, and universally send rockets into outer space. M.I.T.'s is not the graceful and aristocratic architecture of Harvard or the University of Virginia, or the environmentally reverent architecture of California's Santa Cruz, for neither an eighteenth-century sense of decorum nor a nineteenth-century sense of nature can express twentieth-century man's celebration of his own power. As Professor Valley said at a student meeting: "The ancient Greeks trembled in awe before the piteous might of their tribal gods, but the thunderbolts Zeus had to throw around are nothing compared to the power science has put in the hands of modern man."

Impressive as the architecture of power can be when seen on the outside, it must be ignored if one is to overcome the discomfort of living and working in a monument. The interminable gray corridors of the main building invite attack, and as I was walking through them one day, I was explaining to a friend how I thought the campus expressed the Institute's sense of values. A graduate student, who was walking down the corridor slightly ahead of us, overheard my analysis and turned to comment: "You don't understand. I don't even notice these halls any more." I responded by saying that the very fact that his education forced him to move, with a split consciousness, in absolute indifference to his environment required a higher psychic price than he was, perhaps, aware of. The price might seem small to him, but when his attitude was multiplied by all the other engineers in our industrial culture, it became evident in the polluted environment and the Cape

Kennedy neurotic family life of engineers in what psychiatrists call "the aerospace syndrome."[1] Still persisting in thinking that I was merely talking about the prettification of the countryside, the student concluded by saying, as he accelerated down the corridor, "I came here to build computers. The question is not how to appreciate the environment, but how to master it." If I had stuffed words into a straw man's mouth, I could not have created a better expression of the M.I.T. culture of power.

The graduate student was not unique. Many M.I.T. students are quick to dismiss the relevance of the past to man's new mastery, for as another student remarked: "Man now dominates nature." This sense of technological mastery over nature, and the internal contradictions contained in it, are nowhere so brilliantly expressed on campus as in I. M. Pei's Earth Sciences Building. The tallest building in Cambridge, its twenty-odd stories spring from its incredibly narrow and costly alluvial-basin foundation to demonstrate that a modern building can do without its first two floors to stand mightily upon two sides and four slender pylons. With its missing floors given over to an open archway, the building strides the courtyard like a colossus while we petty mortals peep about its legs and marvel at the power of M.I.T. and American technology in general. In keeping with its celebration of man over nature, the building spurns the natural light, which comes to it unobstructedly on both sides, and protects the heating and air-conditioning systems by shutting out the daylight with bronzed windows. On the few sunny days of a Cambridge winter, the sun is blurred, and on the brightest noon of summer electric light can be seen burning behind the darkened glass.

It is an experience to stare upward at the building, but for two years it has also been a dangerous one. The ambitiously calculated stresses have caused the costly dark windows to crack, and M.I.T. has had to suffer the ignominy of having to rope off the courtyard to protect its students from the work of one of its graduates. But even that wasn't the final irony. Skyscraper that it is, the building obstructs enough air to send the wind funneling through its legs. The old doors could not be opened by the secretaries and huge black metal revolving doors had to be installed at the cost of the original boldness of the design. Nature found its revenge on this Earth Sciences Building in a poetic way. Had the first two floors not been proudly omitted, the wind would not have been able to funnel through. So, much like a Greek tragic hero, it was only in striving so high that the building encountered its nemesis.

The building is M.I.T.'s symbol. On a personal level, it shows what M.I.T. training does to students from foreign cultures. A traditional Chinese, filled with the Tao, would never have forgotten earth, wind, and light to design such an embarrassing monument to the study of the earth. In soaring so high, and in straining so hard for Western values, the building renders visible the internal contradictions of Pei's genius, for, as Marx pointed out, it is only at the moment of furthest development that the internal contradictions of an institution, a country, or an age can be seen. So it is now with our technological civilization. In the seventeenth century we took a turn into what Alfred North Whitehead calls "scientific materialism" and introduced a whole new readjustment of the mind's relationship with nature; now the effects of that readjustment are becoming visible, tragically visible.

In the Greek sense of tragedy a man's unique excellence (*areté*) is identical with his tragic flaw (*hamartia*). Achilles will not survive the Christian surgery that would remove his pride but keep his heroic grandeur and courage. So it is with M.I.T. and modern technological man in general: our technology is at once our unique excellence and our tragic flaw. We have the power to send our huge jets into the upper atmosphere, where the tons of pollutants they spew can do far more damage than they ever could if they flew closer to the earth. We have the economic power to create an affluent, richly applianced middle class through massive government support of industry, but as that power races toward increasing prosperity through the manufacture of thousands of SST jets, it is also racing toward eliminating the earth's atmosphere. We have the power to mass-produce the automobiles that make our large cities possible, and now our cities are choking in smog and becoming themselves engines of internal combustion. Oblivious to Van Allen Belts around the earth and Rouse Belts within the earth, we have exploded hydrogen bombs in the earth's magnetic field and are now exploding them in its faulty Pacific crust. And from recent minor military tinkering with our environment we have had man-made earthquakes in Colorado, the nerve-gas annihilation of thousands of sheep in Utah, and the phosgene-gas accidents in

Mississippi. The technology that brilliantly succeeded for two centuries by moving in complete indifference to nature now seems about to suffer massive retaliation.[2]

Technologists, of course, have not been raised on Greek tragedy; they will not accept the fact that their unique excellence and their tragic flaw are one, and so they brush the warnings aside as early technological problems that later technologies will take care of. To be sure, antigravity and flying saucers might solve the problems of roads, automobiles, and jets, but that technological millennium seems much farther off than the new 500-horsepower cars and the President's approval of the SST and the ABM. Perhaps, while the engineer lurches forward into his future, those of us who are not owned by the wealth of the industrial system would do well to step to the side and look back at that seventeenth-century turn that has brought us into our present dead end.

Modern science triumphed over medieval alchemy by eliminating the mind's affective resonance with nature. Roger Bacon thought his alembic was a microcosm of the mountains at large, and that if his mind were as focused in his laboratory as God's was in His creation, then he would be able to move with nature in its teleological process and raise base metals higher in the Chain of Being to become gold. In Latin, "laboratory" means a place to work and pray. But alchemy didn't *work,* and nature had to be deadened before it could become a tool to our ends. We conquered the superstition that kept us chanting litanies on our knees in front of nature, only now to be brought down to them again by the overtowering *hybris* that moves in utter contempt for the very ecology that supports human life. Those of us who, as teachers of the humanities, stand in the chorus but never touch the *skēnē* of action, can see the tragedy coming, but it does no good to shout a warning to the hero. He cannot hear us, for he moves in a world apart, distracted from his surroundings by his past successes and his own invincible sense of power. Man and the humanities are out of his hearing, except on state occasions when atavisms are decorative and lip service is paid to "the education of the whole man." The engineer, be he capitalist or Communist, has been *trained* to his success, not his failure, and he will continue to perform according to his training until the diastrous end. Then the inconceivable will be obvious, civilizaton will scream, and the world will turn over. Since each age is the reversal of the last, I would hope that over the ashes of the old technology a new Whiteheadian science could arise.

But the disasters that will change the M.I.T. world view will not be merely ecological, for if that were the case, we all could think our lifetimes might just make it to this side of apocalypse. No, the disasters will be, and are already, on all fronts: ecological, social, political, psychological, moral, and spiritual. When men are trained to strive for power over their environment, they are socially constrained to achieve that success through a suppression of consciousness in which ambiguity, complexity, feeling, intuition, and imagination are dismissed as irrelevant distractions. Students who raise intellectual questions about some of the ideas in physics are told to forget about them and concentrate on finishing the problem sets. Since there is no room allowed for the imagination in physics, one can surmise how small a living space the young engineer is asked to develop in.

And this is what "the aerospace syndrome" is all about. Operating with a strictly logical and mechanistic model of the self, M.I.T. training reduces the self's truly complex nature to a few relatively standard industrial functions. Such intense specialization enables men to become highly successful within their own corporate structures, for these also collectively suppress what they individually lack, and so no one notices as they all limp along with half an organism. But once these men marry, their inability to deal with the larger nature of consciousness incapacitates them in the demanding relationship with wives and children. To be a success in our industrial culture means, almost of necessity, that a man must be a bad husband and father. Inevitably, the trained man grows to resent his wife and children and thinks that the fault is theirs because they are illogical and not as superior as he is because they lack his training. Thus, to adopt William Hazlitt's metaphor, M.I.T. training fits its students for their future like beggars who maim their children so that they can become successful beggars.

The difference between the expressive nature of education and the repressive nature of training is seen in the pattern that psychiatrists have observed in the family life of professional people. Our ordinary social reaction is to dismiss the high incidence of neurotic disorders as beside the point of the fine work our engineers are doing in putting man on the moon, but such a dismissal is *prima facie* evidence of the dehumanization technological training encourages. It is frivolous, we are told, to attack so great a piece of reality as M.I.T. on the basis of mere family disturbances, because it is better that the father damage his family than have the family damage his work. In one is a backyard barbecue or a day with the Little League, but in the other is the defense of the nation and the conquest of space. Such a shortsighted defense, however, overlooks the long-range problems that are threatening the planet and not just the nation.

In a man's relation with his wife and children he realizes parts of himself. If an individual is a severely damaged person, he will naturally have difficulty with the child who represents the part of himself he has destroyed for success. Inevitably, he will seek through force and excessive discipline to restrict the threat of that child's free development. One of the most brilliant students I encountered at M.I.T. was a girl who came from a socially distinguished and wealthy family; like many other freshmen she reacted to her impeccable background by smoking pot, reading unacceptable books, and wearing unacceptable clothes. Her middle-aged father responded with a voyeurism in which he opened her mail, slapped her on the face in confrontations, called her "evil," and disowned her as a disgrace to the family fortune. The incident is significant because this response has become the national one. Ironically, our advanced technologies of education, child-rearing, and police control seem to have brought us back to the mythic situation in which Cronus tries to devour his children and the children think that if they castrate their fathers they will be free.

Because family life is supremely difficult for a man who has been trained in the M.I.T. fashion, it is more than likely that "The Technological Society" will respond to the crisis of the traditional family by eliminating altogether this source of anxiety for our productive engineers. The present technology has already lessened the importance of parents in child-rearing, for no parent can control the information that floods through the home. "The home" itself is an atavistic notion lingering on in our new untraditional high-rise culture, for no parents, rich or poor, can alter the fact that children grow up in age sets and that the new media-created envelopment of youth culture is their new home. Since we are already living in the age of the media kibbutzim, it will only be a short step to have the behavioral engineers solve the problems of the broken families of the blacks and the dropout families of the whites by eliminating altogether familial sexuality in procreation.[3]

We are already well advanced on the road of seeking a technological answer for all difficult problems, and although we have not yet perfected the science of electronic behavioral therapy, we are making do with some temporary forms of psychotherapy that adjust the individual to "life" in a technological society. The psychiatric clinic at M.I.T. is one of the largest and most advanced of its kind in any American university. One evening one of the resident psychiatrists gave a talk to the humanities faculty in which he explained to us how he handled the problem of the student who was losing his way through the gray corridors of M.I.T. When a student became dissatisfied with what he was doing, he would suggest to

him that he leave school for a while to work for
VISTA or some civil rights program in the South.
Having rediscovered a sense of purpose in an environment in which the issues of civilization were etched
in deep relief, then, it was hoped, the student would
be able to carry his ideals back with him to continue
his education.

The psychiatrist's talk was a perfect exposure of
the Eastern liberal: evil was something that existed
down in the South, where those hideous rednecks who
did not revere the professional class were holding
down an oppressed but noble and inspiring people.
Armies have been known to import whores to keep
the soldiers going, but here was an even more
imaginative form of moral harlotry: one inserted one's
conscience into the South, did a few things, finished
off, and withdrew to one's former life relieved. And
just as once the lower-class whore stopped the young
aristocrat from discovering that women of his own
station had female bodies, so now the mythopoeic
descent of the engineer into the South stops him from
seeing that evil exists at M.I.T. and that, in fact, it
may be just that evil which is causing him to lose
his way.

M.I.T. needs a large psychiatric clinic because the
effect of technological training is to do to the psyche
what industry does to the environment. Since few
men willingly suffer their own dehumanization, industry and technology have found that an appeal to
sexuality is one very efficient way of camouflaging the
internal and external dehumanization. The industrial
quality of sexuality is, of course, clearly in evidence
in the ads in *Playboy,* the best-selling magazine in

the Tech Coop. In a penthouse apartment that is a technological paradise of stereos, tape recorders, cameras, blenders, automatic bars, and electric beds, the sleek air-brushed nude that offers enjoyment without involvement is the ideal appliance of any young engineer's dream. Producing sensations wtihout sentience, the female represents what every trained technologist desires. He is free to dismiss everything that his culture tells him to, and still be safe from the exposure that personal involvement with a real woman might contain. He is free to exploit her in a fantasy of phallic dominance, or in the words of an ad that shows a rampant stallion as emblem of its cologne: "Use Stud. Make her cry a little." And what the adolescent engineer rehearses in miniature in his fantasied relations with women, he is even freer to do at large with nature, for the instictive play of our technology is the exploitation of passive, female nature in a celebration of power and phallic dominance.

In keeping with this sexual mythology of rational male dominance over irrational female nature, we have constructed an ideology of progress that places our industrial culture at the pinnacle of human civilization. A recent letter to the *Playboy* "Forum" expresses this American idea of progress in the following way:

Say all you want about the physical harmlessness of marijuana, its mental effects seem to be almost always incompatible with our kind of progressive, technological civilization. Almost every engineering student I've known who started using grass regularly soon switched to a liberal-arts college, where he took up philosophy and Oriental mysticism and—in many cases—got hooked on the Chinese *I Ching* bit, Hindu reincarnation philosophy, American Indian prophecies and visions or some harmless, charming but worthless nonsense. Pot smokers don't become vicious, depraved dope fiends, but they certainly will not contribute anything toward beating the Russians in the space race, curing cancer, or advancing science and industry in any way.[4]

In the mind of this young engineer "science and industry" is one word and human progress is a sales chart in a corporation board room in which history is reduced to a single line that begins with the wheel and ends with the bomb. To see history in this way we have to close our eyes to anything that would disturb our pre-eminence, but since we are trained to dismiss history as irrelevant to man's new power, this blindness is part of our way of looking at things. And yet if we can learn anything from the ruins of Stonehenge and Yucatán, it is that technologies are too vastly different and complex to be compared with one another on a simple linear scale by which we judge others with our own values. The acoustical engineering at the Ball Court at Chichén Itzá is superior to that of M.I.T.'s Kresge Auditorium, or any other building in America. And the mathematical and astronomical sophistication of the stone computers at Stonehenge and the Caracole at Chichén Itzá belie anything resembling primitiveness. But because these are not industrial civilizations we tend to dismiss their fantastic accomplishments as the products of slaves laboring under the misguided fantasies of a class of high priests. We never stop to consider what a future civilization might make of the engineers and workers at Ford who labor to put more sex appeal into the new Mustang.

History is not a line but a dial. If you stand at the center of the dial and face toward six o'clock, you have to turn your back on midnight. At midnight is the music, mathematics, and spirituality of the science of Pythagoras, science we no longer understand; at six o'clock is the industrial technology in which we live. But now as the hand sweeps around, it is growing later and later, and once again we are having to face our opposite to look toward dark midnight. Each technology activates certain human possibilities and pays the price for ignoring their opposites, which is another way of saying that the unique excellence and the tragic flaw are one and inseparable.

We don't know what happened to the people of Stonehenge in 1400 B. C. and why they abandoned their center. Mystical in the extreme, the people must have been our exact mirror opposite; but all that astronomical wizardry and sensitivity to nature did little good when a climatic change made the observatory useless through fogged-in skies, or so one theory goes. The Mayas, too, were creators of a culture with a poetry of mathematics and a cosmic vision of the stars that would dwarf the awareness of most engineers. They could cover Middle America with huge pyramids and still not use the wheel; they could calculate star positions back millions of years, but still not have metal weapons. The bill came due for these people because the Pythagorean elite ignored the industrial base of society and calculated star positions, but forgot the peasant's religion of growing corn.

But, as George Wallace has recently pointed out, elites do not have to be permanent; and so the monuments were disfigured and the ceremonial centers were attacked, disfigured, and abandoned, and the peasants went back to their religion of the fertile earth. Now we are playing out the other side of the circle, and in exact inverse correspondence we are ignoring the Pythagorean consciousness of nature to expand our industrial base. Understandably, the peasants of our technological society, the students, are disfiguring the monuments and attacking the ceremonial centers.

Progress is a myth falser than any of the true myths of our history. Our celebrated technology realizes great human possibilities, but we are paying a great price for them, and with every year the price keeps going up. We are literally sick of and sick with the phallic culture of our industrial technology. For years business exploited and excited sexuality to sell everything from cars to cigars, little realizing that Eros and Thanatos are inseparable, and that you can't excite the one without provoking reactions in the other. The adolescent who was sold his Honda by an ad in *Playboy* that showed it parting the thighs of a bikini-clad girl is the same man who is now socking it to female Asia in his bullet-spurting gunship. The marine who was taught to chant "This is my rifle and this is my gun; one is for fighting, the other for fun" and "What is the spirit of the bayonet? To kill!" is the same marine who climbed the tower of the University of Texas to shoot forth his power on the passers-by. The phallic culture of our industrial civilization begins with the toy guns of little boys, develops into the puberty rites of car and motorcycle, and climaxes in the technological rape of Vietnam. But, of course, we are told by our behavioral scientists whose research is financed by the government, all these things are separate and unrelated. The family life of engineers, the fantasies of adolescent men, the sexuality of advertising, all these have nothing to do with the whole technological culture of America.

If there is a danger in taking the caricatures of the mass media too seriously, there is no danger in taking education seriously. Yet here again one encounters the sexual imagery that is taken from the larger mythological envelopments of advertising. Although the sexual play of our technology is blatant in the extreme in the media, it is more subtle in education, for M.I.T. has four years to work on the individual's mind; a commercial has only a few seconds. Yet even in the high seriousness of technological training one finds the same mythological obsessions running through speeches and lectures.

A case in point was the symposium held at the Institute in dedication of its new Center for Advanced Visual Studies (read art). Otto Piene, M.I.T.'s artist in residence, said that he felt uneasy at this shotgun marriage of art and technology and did not know whether he was the bride or the groom. The proceedings cleared away any doubt about the receptive nature of art. As one engineer said at the meeting: "We can make things that work but aren't beautiful. The artist can make things that are beautiful but don't work." The engineers naïve male-female ideas of technology and art were quickly challenged by Piene, who recalled the nineteenth-century marriage of art and technology which produced rose-decorated sewing machines. Another engineer from Bell Telephone Laboratories described a more up-to-date means by which technology could help the artist. He showed that we now possess the skill to place probes on a man's head and induce pleasant sensations in response to, say, the image of a woman on a screen. At last technological man could dispense with woman altogether to have an electronic orgasm in a geodesic dome, and while the sun was being obscured by the SST haze in the upper atmosphere and the earth was losing solar radiation, man could crawl back into the cave where industrial shamans could throw latrine images on the walls.

The guilty technologists had destroyed the environment; now their servile apologists, the technocratic artists, were trying to make up for it in an environmental art. One could almost hear the bureaucratic apologists discussing pollution at another future symposium at M.I.T.: "Although the spin-off from our technology has caused undesired consequences *through inadequately funded research and development* for habitational systems contiguous to the productive sector, we can be grateful that the forward thrust of that technology has given us the means to stay on top of the problem with relative ease. The artificial life-support systems that were designed for our astronauts in the sixties have given us the knowledge to create whole new environments in civilized containers of the geodesic variety. Surely, if we can keep man alive on the moon, or in the bottom of the sea, keeping him alive in Cambridge should prove no real problem."

When our technology becomes sufficiently advanced, and our cities sufficiently disintegrated, that technologists are ready to declare martial law to solve the problems they have created and move man into flourescent-lit and acoustically tiled containers, then we will witness the largest nativistic revolution in history. For whether it is Moses, Amos, Padraic Pearse, or Malcolm X, the prophet of the nativistic movement is the man who can summon precivilized energies to overcome the threats of extreme urbanization. When, therefore, the technologists propose that we leave the planet to their industrial scum, then the earth will split apart in a conflict between nativists and technocrats, and the history of all the revitalization movements of the past will be consummated in continuous technological repression (with its concomitant hedonism) and continuous guerrilla, antitechnological warfare. If we let things go on until they become that desperate, we may find ourselves in that tragic kind of conflict in which both sides are wrong. A merely political revolution without a change in our technological world view is homicidal; a religious transformation that excludes science is atavistic and suicidal. We somehow have to outflank the ignorant armies of the Left and Right to find the space and time to convert our industrial technology to a new kind of Pythagorean science. Given the current mentality of the United States, Canada would seem to be the last space and time North America has left.

In this cultural transformation of North America,

the scientists and the humanists will have to work together to deflect the engineers and the behavioral scientists from the disasters they have set up as the goals of our technological civilization. In the eyes of the physicist Werner Heisenberg, our very strength has now become a weakness.

With the seemingly unlimited expansion of his material might, man finds himself in the position of a captain whose ship has been so securely built of iron and steel that the needle of his compass no longer points to the north, but only toward the ship's mass of iron. With such a ship no destination can be reached; it will move aimlessly and be subject in addition to winds and ocean currents. But let us remember the state of affairs in modern physics: the danger only exists so long as the captain is unaware that his compass does not respond to the earth's magnetic forces. The moment the situation is recognized, the danger can be considered as half removed. For the captain who does not want to travel in circles, but desires to reach a known—or unknown—destination will find ways and means for determining the orientation of the ship. He may start using modern types of compasses that are not affected by the iron of the ship, or he may navigate, as in former times, by the stars. Of course we cannot decree the visibility or lack of visibility of the stars, and in our time perhaps they are only rarely visible. In any event, awareness that the hopes engendered by the belief in progress will meet a limit implies the wish not to travel in circles but to reach a goal. To the extent that we reach clarity about this limit, the limit itself may furnish the first firm hold by which we can orient ourselves anew.

Perhaps from this comparison with modern science we may draw hope that we may be here dealing with a limit for certain forms of expansion of human activity, not, however, with a limit to human activity as such.

The space in which man as a spiritual being is developing has more dimensions than the one within which he has moved in the preceding centuries. It follows that in the course of long stretches of time the conscious acceptance of this limit will perhaps lead to a certain stabilization in which the thoughts of men will again arrange themselves around a common center. Such a development may perhaps also supply a new foundation for the development of art; but to speak about that does not behoove the scientist.[5]

M.I.T. has not yet realized that its needle is only pointing in the direction of its own iron mass; it still thinks it is going somewhere and is confidently hoping to lead civilization in its direction. In the expensive symposium in dedication of the new Center, M.I.T. was not trying to listen to the artists but was trying to beguile them with all the temptations at its disposal. The technocrats were seeking to convert the artists into new celebrants of the system; in making a technological art possible, they were insuring the stability of their technological society.

In preindustrial culture art is the handmaiden of religion; in some cultures, like the Balinese, art is so much a part of an all-pervasive way of life that the people can say: "We have no art; we do everything as well as we can." But in the industrial culture of the nineteenth century, people were profound only while in front of a symphony or a painting; or, for the refugees from bourgeois culture, in a peasant cottage or on top of a lofty prospect. To insure that the aesthetic experience stayed in its place to leave the landscape free for industrial development, the painting was locked in a huge restraining gilt frame,[6] and the individual was locked in evening dress or business suit while he watched theatrical imitations of reality in the privacy of his anonymous darkness.

All that is over, and now we have the withering away of art in the posthistoric landscape. The painting has spilled over its edges to involve the whole environment, and with the environment as the new work of art (McLuhan), painting and sculpture have retreated into the stripes and minimal forms of what is really only interior decoration (painting) or punctuation marks (sculpture) in the complex narrative of urban spaces. Music has spilled out of the orchestra to involve the body in configurations of light and color, and for pot-awakened ears, listening itself has become the real performance. With computers replacing instruments and performers, we, too, can paraphrase the Balinese to say: "We have no art; we do as little as we can."

Literature, too, has taken part in this cultural transformation, for the novel which grew up with the urban classes (and therefore always possessed their work ethic) has given way to the film and the anti-novel. Reading itself (and especially the *work* of reading nine-hundred-page novels) is becoming an antique, ritualized performance. The *new* art of a Godard or a Robbe-Grillet breaks from the past by no longer having *material*. When the traditional Cartesian reality was split between subject and object, *matter,* when subjectively formed or decorated, constituted art. Now we have moved beyond that "bifurcated universe" into one of "process," where "events" themselves become the "occasions" for art. Be-ins, love-ins, happenings, guerrilla theater, political demonstrations, trials, encounter groups—all indicate that avant-garde art is simply the scaffolding that one takes down when the edifice of the Revolution is raised. The ultimate performance of this newly emerging metapersonal consciousness is the Revolution, but this Revolution should not be confused with mere political upheavals, be they Russian, Chinese, Cuban, or American. These, too, are only rehearsals for the complete transformation of basic human nature and civilization.

This quantum leap in human cultural evolution, of course, cannot come without dislocating the old individual. For the artist, there is the crisis of his talent and its relevance. Before, reality lent metaphors to the artist, and from Napoleon's wars Tolstoy could steal a novel. Now, in the technological era, the situation is reversed and reality is borrowing patterns from the entertainers first and Norman Mailer second. When the landscape was disappearing because of industrialization, Wordsworth and the other romantics lifted it up into art. Now that NASA has given us a lunar perspective of the planet, the environment has become the work of art and the body and the mind have become our new form of landscape.

But technology is not only invading nature and outer space; it has also begun its invasion of our sensual bodies. The body is now a native reservation in which ancient man is being kept out of the way of our advancing technological civilization. In face of the machine, man now affirms his humanity in nudity, sexuality, and the polymorphous sensuousness of Esalen. Scientists now speak openly about the obsolete nature of the body and childbirth. Since evidence points to the fact that male animals raised without physical mothers prove to be impotent as adults, it is only a question of perhaps a century or less before Homo Sexualis takes his place with Homo Neanderthalensis. But as things sense their disappearance, they find their most elaborate artistic expression. The brightest colors are reserved for sunset and that is why we are now in the midst of a "sexual explosion." Child-bearing is about to become the ritual-art of the affluent classes, as breast-feeding is now. Romantics will play at being Mother and Father, but the mass will probably express itself in ways that we ancient men would find polymorphously perverse.

McLuhan says that artists are early-warning devices that describe the nature of the invisible environment in which we live. The emphasis, then, on oral intercourse in all the new books (*Beautiful Losers, Couples, Love's Body*), the new plays (*The Beard, Futz,* and *Che*), and the new films (*Bonnie and Clyde, Masculine Feminine, The Magus, I Am Curious*) is an overpopulated world's "displacement upward" which describes the diffusely sensual and androgynous quality of sexuality in the emerging post-childbearing era. Breast and penis become indistinguishable as they become one oral gratification. As the breast is turned into an intrusive phallus, and the daggerlike phallus of the old male is turned into a lactating breast, the ancient roles of Mother and Father disappear and "man" is succeeded by the androgynous angel or demon. These new bisexual mutants have already appeared on the cultural evolutionary scene, and the fact that Mick Jagger, Andy Warhol, and Jim Morrison are pop idols of youth culture indicates that the generation gap between the industrial parents and the postindustrial kids is far wider than the grownups realize. As things seem to be going now, the gap will widen, and when the grownups realize just how deeply "the new mutants" reject their whole assumptions about the nature of being human, their attack on the young will reach saturnine proportions.

What appears to be going on in this transformation of human nature is in many ways a technological parody of Genesis. In the too often overlooked brilliance of the Biblical myth, the condition of being human is seen in man's language and his sexuality. Variant Hebrew myths describe how man triumphed over the critical angels because he could *name* the animals in God's procession of the creatures.[7] The angels, evidently, lacked a verbal consciousness. But for all his power of "the word" that man possessed in the image of God, he still fell, for he looked on the copulating animals and desired to be like them. Adam, the original androgyne, desired to be split into male and female. The cell is asexual and immortal; the organism is sexual and dies. When Adam and Eve fell, time and history began, for in becoming sexual there was no other way of experience except through the knowledge of good (Eros) and evil (Thanatos).

The inextricable weaving of love and death is the condition of being human; it is, therefore, no wonder that as technologists seek to eliminate sexuality in procreation, they are also hard at work on biological immortality. Every humanist knows that sex and death make us what we are, and that all human civilization is completely destroyed without them; but what we are now is not what the technologists would have us become. The Technological Revolution is about to reverse the curse of Genesis so that man shall no longer have to earn his bread by the sweat of his brow and woman shall no longer bring forth children in pain and sorrow. Work is dying, sex is dying, and even bread is dying, for the industrialized foods of the supermarket are taking us beyond the world of taste and the fruits of nature into the zombie-foods of the astronauts, Tang, Wonder Bread, and Carnation Instant Breakfast. The transformation will not pain modern mass man, for given the power of M.I.T.'s behavioral engineering and the techniques of its Sloan School of Management, he will look at the thousands of bright packages and really think there is a wonderful freedom of choice in the twenty different brands of bad bread available to him.

The techniques that will be used on the population at large are already in the experimental stage at M.I.T., not in gruesome laboratories where live brains in jars respond to electronic probes, but in classrooms where unsuspecting teachers and students find new areas in which technology can help us to live a richer life. In the old days of industrial engineering, the technologists barely tolerated the presence of artists and humanists on the faculty, but now in the age of behavioral engineering, they are indeed welcome, for art and the humanities are just those areas in which the good intentions of the technocrats can be displayed.

It is fitting that, in the Technological Revolution that is hopefully to take us from a culture of meaningless work to one of meaningful play, the sculptural forms of contemporary art should have the oversize shape, minimal form, and brilliant colors of nursery toys. For in turning away from "the genital organization" it is only natural that the first movement should be a regression to infantile sexuality. And it was exactly this kind of infantile art that came to the gray corridors of M.I.T. First we had technology-art in which the displays from freshman physics underwent an apotheosis—stripes, op, pop, and·minimal. Then the climax of the season came with the exhibition of the Park Place Group, a cooperative of New York-based painters and sculptors. To say, then, that this Park Place art is infantile is to take hold of the thing. The only difficulty with this particular style is that it is not so much postgenital, postindustrial, postbourgeois, as simply antibourgeois. The artists are only a mirror image of the bourgeoisie; take away the burgher's face from the mirror, and the artist's face disappears too. And that is, perhaps, one reason these artists and the bourgeoisie understand one another so well in the bullish marketplace of art.

By contrast with these gallery pieces of art, the minimal forms of a real playground are true sensuous forms, for these you can touch, crawl over, kick, swing on, and dirty. If you were to try that with one of "the Park Place minimals," a police officer would be quick to inform you that they cost at a bare minimum so many thousands of dollars. In short, the art is a fraud of the liberal-apologists that its admirers so richly deserve. And that art will remain a fraud until the forms have become the inexpensive creations of anonymous artisans placed in parks for the complete enjoyment of children and adults. But until such a time this art will remain in the galleries to lend a little class to ambitious institutions where bureaucrats are busily engaged in humanization programs—programs likely to be as successful as pacification in Vietnam.

The conflict between the artists and the apologists is not restricted to the department of art, but is expressive of the larger conflict of the Institute and society in general. As a large institution, M.I.T., like others of its postwar variety, is run by specialists in the management of large institutions; it is run by men of operational rather than ideational temperament. Before Howard Johnson took his post as president he had accepted the presidency of a large chain of department stores. Men who are specialists in the management of complex organizations learn quite early that the best way to preserve the stability of powerful routines is to give on the surface the illusion of reform and constant innovation. The symposium which celebrated the new M.I.T. with its Centers for Advanced Visual Studies and Theoretical Physics was just such brilliant camouflage for the "military-industrial complex." But for years the greatest producer of camouflage has been the Department of Humanities.

M.I.T. likes to tell its visitors that one-third of a student's time is spent in the humanities; which is true if you consider, as the Institute does, economics as a branch of the humanities. By this clever definition the public relations men are able to generalize a single required freshman course into an entire program in which the new engineer rivals the effete

Harvard English major in a knowledge of Plato, Thucydides, and Homer. The importance of such advertising is that it helps to soften M.I.T.'s hard image as a technical school and to woo back bright students who might turn down- the Institute to go to Harvard or Yale. Moreover, the emphasis on art and the humanities helps maintain M.I.T.'s self-image as an upper-class institution with its concern for what Julius Stratton, the previous president, called "taste and the first-rate." M.I.T. was one of the first American schools to break away from the traditional education of a gentleman to suggest that engineering need not be considered hopelessly Midwestern and middle-class. It is, therefore, essential that it not slip into the vulgarity of the trade-school education of more lower-middle-class schools of technology which look up to M.I.T. Of course, the proximity to Harvard has helped keep the social competition keen. So, like Muzak in a factory, the Department of Humanities has proven how a seemingly frivolous thing can serve its purpose in increasing over-all productivity. But the situation is not novel, for when the Romans were busy conquering the world, they liked to keep educated Greek slaves around to lend a little class to their operations.

This triumph of the technocratic, operational mentality at M.I.T. has come about through the successful transplanting of the image-making techniques from advertising to education. The public relations men reason that there is an M.I.T. style and that this style should be reflected throughout all the departments. According to the PR men, if at M.I.T. biology is molecular, psychology is the physiology of the brain, and political science is computer-generated biostatistics, then it follows that if the humanities and art can show imaginative ways of giving up their atavistic inclinations, funds will be found to turn philosophy into information theory, history into the comparative modernization of the Third World, and literature into linguistics. Since an M.I.T. humanist is looked down upon as an overblown high school teacher, the prospect of receiving enough money to support majors in technologized humanities and possibly even graduate students makes him feel that he finally has a chance "to stand as tall" as his colleagues in the behavioral sciences. And so the faculty member soon finds that he is not working alone out there at the frontiers of knowledge, for looking over his shoulder is a PR man who is musing to himself that the work may be all right elsewhere, "But is it really the M.I.T. Way of Doing Things?" Inevitably, as happens in all large bureaucracies, the operational members, who are supposed to be there to assist the ideational men in the real work of a university, end up by telling them how to think as well as act.

The humanist at M.I.T thus finds himself in a situation that is no doubt prophetic of the condition of the citizen in the technological society of the *magnus annus*, A.D. 2000. To the degree that the humanist succeeds in technologizing the humanities (by turning them into the social sciences), he destroys the humanities; to the degree that he ignores the technological world and teaches as one might at Cardinal Newman's Oxford, he ensures the conviction in his students' minds that the humanities are simply irrelevant to the mastery of our new complex society; to the degree that he succeeds in communicating the relevance of the traditional humanities to our society, he finds himself welcomed by the administration as valuable camouflage, and resented by his students, who correctly point out that while he makes a great noise, he is still powerless to affect the inhumane training of the whole Institute. The naïve humanist thinks that in teaching the humanities to M.I.T. students he is helping a major American institution deal with the problems of our civilization, but it does not take long for the students to educate the teacher to see that the Institute is, as Eldridge Cleaver would say, not part of the solution, but part of the problem.

But the liberal bureaucrats eventually got their just desserts; for it was psychologically inevitable that an environment drenched with the lust for power would generate its opposite in the form of radicals. In one of those sudden advertising transformations that is supposed to turn an old-fashioned department into a modernized M.I.T. discipline, literature was to turn into linguistics. But at M.I.T. linguistics means Noam Chomsky, the nation's leading academic radical, and so the new style of literary scholarship was not about to become an image-making device for the bureaucrats. Almost overnight, Chomsky's political associate, Louis Kampf, was able to turn a colorless literature division into the leading radical English department in the country. If the attempt to marry technology and art had produced only a sterile mule, there still was a chance that M.I.T. might just bring off a fruitful union this time, and, with Chom-

sky's theories of mind to strengthen the exhausted
state of English, produce one of the most vigorously
intellectual departments in the nation.

Unfortunately, so bourgeois a vision of mere intellectual change never had a chance; the importance
of the humanities at M.I.T. was not that they provided a space free of academic stultification, but that
they provided a space for guerrilla theater right in the
vitals of the military-industrial-academic complex.
The lust for power of the technocrats had not created
a contrary situation, but had only generated a Shadow
Establishment equally consumed by the same lust.
Precisely because the radicals were so busy pulling
and tugging with all their might at the means of production and distribution, they could not see that they
shared the same technological world view: what the
liberals loved and the radicals hated equally possessed
them both.

In the rush of political action there was no time to
investigate the rich possibilities that Chomsky's
theories of language and mind offer to the study of
literature. It was a great opportunity that was missed,
for the radicals are articulate in attacking the fatu-
ousness of conservative literary scholarship[8] and the
arrogant stupidity of the liberal behavioral sciences.[9]
Chomsky has written the classic refutation of behaviorism and has given the humanists new ammunition
in their war against the dehumanization contained
in the manipulative ideology of the social sciences.
Since social scientists read one another's reprints
but do not read Plato, Descartes, Vico, Kant, much
less Coleridge, Chomsky is telling them things they
don't know. But for humanists, much of Chomsky

is simply a modern notation for very traditional ideas. Ironically, most of these ideas of the universal grammar of the mind are part of the conservative and romantic tradition; they lead more in the direction of Burke than in the materialist direction of Chomsky's New Left.

Although the New Left has its brilliant intellectuals like Chomsky, and its stern Old Left moralists like Kampf, too many in the movement are simply possessed with cant, rancor, hate and a crowd zeal for thought-circumventing action. Anything that is not on the revolutionary's side in the castration of the father is simply thought to be on the side of Uranus or irrelevant to the historical situation, which he defines as the necessity for castration. Freed by his Marxist materialism of the feudal nobility that would suggest that evil is within the revolutionary and his movement as well as outside himself in capitalist society, he rages in a blindness that prevents him from seeing the vices of his friends and the virtues of his enemies.

Day after day in encounters with M.I.T. radicals, one is subjected to a suspicion of the past that amounts to a willfully self-imposed ignorance: "I won't teach Autobiography and Identity because the self is a bourgeois personalist fiction." "Aeschylus' *Eumenides* is just stupid." "The *Bacchae* is a bad play because there is no central character who expresses a sympathetic ideology." "What is there to say about Wordsworth except that he tried to make nature into a *religion,* and that only takes an hour, so why waste a week on him?" The radicals can be incisive in pointing out the ethnocentricity of "The

Great Tradition" in which ideas are wrenched out of
their cultural context and arranged in a pseudo-
historical narrative of Bible, Augustine, Dante, Shakespeare, Pascal, Pope, Wordsworth, Lawrence, Joyce,
and Eliot, a narrative that embalms the books until
all they are fit for is the decorative and untouched
shelf of some suburban stockbroker. But when it is
the radicals' turn to come up with a new curriculum,
all they can think of is Marx, Marcuse, Fanon, and
Cleaver.

The liberal apologists in the humanities, those who
grew up under the joyless bravado of Freud and *The
Future of an Illusion,* respond to the threat of the
radicals to the Tradition by tightening the walls
around it, and the exasperating polarization of American politics becomes reflected in the ideological
battles within the university. As Louis Kampf points
out:

Those wishing to effect the needed radical change
have to organize themselves into a vanguard. Effective-
ness will depend on their union of purpose, on their
capacity to transcend—not necessarily give up—capricious privacies. For the literary intellectual, individualism being a major dogma of his creed, this involves
the most difficult of commitments. Yet we must all
begin to understand that a totally self-centered individualism is not necessarily a sign of heroism or nobility;
it may, in fact, serve as a mask for the complete de-
predations of capitalism. The narcissistic obsession of
modern literature for the self, the critical cant concern-
ing the tragic isolation of the individual—these are
notions which tie our hands and keep us from the
communion necessary for meaningful action.

Another illusion of individualism is a belief in the
efficacy of the charismatic teacher. One cannot be a

great teacher in an evil system. To dazzle students with the brilliance of one's performance and do no more is to submit to the status quo; excelling independently without a concerted program for change, diminishes the possible impact of one's effort; indeed, those concerned primarily with the fulfillment of their egos guarantee the inconsequence of their ideas.[10]

From Kampf's radical point of view, a teacher striving for excellence in teaching is only making a contribution to the life of a university, and thus postponing its necessary death and resurrection. And so in order to prove that the university is dead, the radicals ask us to go about meticulously killing it. In order to prove that there is no morality in the status quo, they label morality a bourgeois personalism which ties our hands and keeps us from meaningful political action. If self-transcendence were really offered by the radicals, then perhaps the sacrifice of one's capricious privacy might be worth it, and by throwing over all the traditions of our bourgeois civilization, we would find salvation in a structureless, anarchic freedom in which polymorphous perversity was reachieved. But both philosophers of liberation, Herbert Marcuse and Norman O. Brown, are wrong. For Marcuse the elimination of solitude is the prelude to a new consolidation in which technological automation will allow us to rid ourselves of the "performance principle" to be erotic forever: eroticism supported by technology is what we already have with *Playboy;* for all his radicalism, Marcuse is a technocrat in disguise. For Brown health and unity come through Eros and a polymorphous anarchism in which the wonder and delight of Logos

and Cosmos are eliminated in a game in which there
are only the two suits of Eros and Thanatos in the
deck. But Brown, for all his luscious temptations,
is satanic. The evocation of Eros is the provocation
of Thanatos, and the transition from one to the other
is always with us and gets us nowhere. Polymorphous
perversity purchased at the price of decapitation
seems something less than Unity of Being. The
elimination of "the genital organization" is really
only a displacement downward of the elimination
of the cerebral organization. In the Luddite hysteria
generated by the Left one begins to suspect that
the radical ideology itself is an example of false
consciousness. The contemporary Technological Revolution is, like the neolithic, a huge cultural transformation in which the radicals are more the erupting
symptoms of the disease than the attending physicians
with the cure.

And so in the double-bind condition created by the
culture of technology, the humanities become either
liberal behavioral science or radical revolutionary
politics; or, in the case of the anarchism of Norman
O. Brown, metapolitics in which we move from
history to mystery. In the first case one has to be a
samurai indifferent to the issues of the battle that
occasions his display of expertise; in the second one
has to be a churl in love with destruction for its own
sake; and in the third, one of the mystai holding the
severed head of Pentheus aloft in a paean of liberation. But there is another kind of anarchism, the kind
which Henry Adams identified as Conservative Christian Anarchism. If the world is fallen and all human
institutions move from the charisma of visionaries

to the routine of bureaucracies, then one must maintain a whimsical sense of irony about the pretensions to perfection of the masters of technique, liberal
or radical. As technocrats and radicals close in upon
one another in a sadomasochistic attraction, one
must move into another space.

In the Middle Ages the point of nature was God;
in the seventeenth century the point generated a line
that moved away from God into the materialism of
nature. Now that line, at its limit, as Heisenberg has
pointed out, must swing into another dimension to
become the radius of a far more inclusive sphere.
At the limit, historical humanism breaks apart and
moves along the circumference in opposite directions of the new extremes of radical Left and radical
Right. But a sphere is two circles at right angles to
one another, and, also at the limit, historical mysticism breaks apart and moves in opposite directions:
down into the demonic transports of Brown's polymorphous anarchism, or up into the Conservative
Christian Anarchism of Henry Adams. Of course we
are all going around in circles, and all the movements are equivalent motions around a center, but,
unfortunately, the political positions turn us around so
that we cannot see that the center is right between
our eyes. The space in which this can be realized
shrinks as Left and Right close in upon us, but
Louis Kampf, in his book *On Modernism,* quoted
Alexander Herzen and pointed a way out of his own
enclosures: "There are times when a man of learn-
ing must withdraw from political and social involvement, from all action, and wait patiently for the
appropriate historical moment."[11]

Now I a fourfold vision see,
And a fourfold vision is given to me;
'Tis fourfold in my supreme delight
And threefold in soft Beulah's night
And twofold Always. May God us keep
From Single vision & Newton's sleep!
WILLIAM BLAKE

4

VALUES AND CONFLICT THROUGH HISTORY:
the view from a Canadian retreat

To understand history, one must stand outside history, not just to avoid bias, but to be able to perceive distinctness and relations. Any simple stand to the Left or the Right is still a movement on the same political plane. But above the American Left and Right is Canada, a place free of the American Dream and the European Nightmare. No longer a colony, not yet an independent national power, Canada, like Switzerland, is *The Peaceable Kingdom*[1] to which those weary of conflict go to escape the burden of a national destiny. As the Canadian historian John Conway has remarked: "America is Faustian and Dionysian; Canada is not." In the opposition between Apollonian Canada and Dionysian America, one can see that once again the unique excellence of both countries is also their tragic flaw. Los Angeles is one very obvious example of an edge, but Toronto is also a city at the edge of American history. With its draft dodgers, deserters, and émigré academics, it is almost Tolkien's Rivendell, safe from the ragings of the archaic darkness of Sauron and the Ring wraiths. Whether one can live permanently in Rivendell is a question I ask myself daily, but at the moment Toronto seems the perfect retreat in which to look from one end of history to the other.

PHASE I. THE TRIBAL COMMUNITY

The historical past with which I wish to begin is not the distant past of the Stone Age, but the archaic present as seen in a classic ethnographic film, John Marshall's *The Hunters*. This film about the Bushmen of South Africa contains not so much the *material* I wish to discuss as the *structure* on which I wish to support a model of the universal form of conflict in values in human institutions. Hidden in the film, as hidden in a fairy tale, is an archetypal structure, a mandala of the species' specific form of human consciousness. Upon the blank screen, Marshall projects his film, and now, like a Chinese box within a box, I would like to project upon the screen of the film a fourfold vision of history.

In the film four men set out from their bush village to hunt for food in an environment that keeps their community always at the edge of starvation. They have no weapons more effective than small arrows tipped with a slow-working poison, and so for them the hunt is a long process in which they must first wound and then trail the animal until it drops. We follow the hunters through many disappointing misses, and then finally they succeed in wounding a giraffe with an arrow. Now the hunt begins in earnest. The men know that it may take more than a week to track the animal to its death, and they know that the whole community behind them depends on what they can bring home. Their previous frivolity drops from them, and the four men move closer together in a finely coordinated pursuit. It is at this point in the film that we begin to see that the men are not just any four, but a very special four. There is the Headman, who is at once the leader of his community and the equal of the men with whom he must hunt. There is one who is called "The Beautiful" and is known for his physical strength, grace, and speed. There is the silent Shaman and craftsman, who works the magic when they have need of it, and there is the Clown, the ugly joker who makes fun of the seriousness of the Shaman, the physical beauty of the best hunter, and the authority of the Headman. They are not just any four men, but four with a very special set of interlocking and complementary qualities.

As they live together for days in pursuit of the giraffe, each man falls into his place and works with the others as if he were the limb of a single organism. And as we watch the four men grow into a stable group under the pressure of the hunt, we come to know them as human beings and not as "primitives." Continually, we are surprised by their amazing skills, for they can read their environment with the attention and understanding of a scientist in his laboratory. From the gathered data of broken twigs and tracks on the shady side of the trees they reason that the poisoned animal is now at the point where the light is hurting his eyes. At one point, Kaow, "The Beautiful," picks up the fallen dung of the giraffe, smells it, and crumbles it in his hand. It is, anthropologically, a beautiful moment in the film, for it always raises laughter and disgust in a student audience. The average student is revolted by his perception of a savage crumbling giraffe dung in his fingers and so he is confirmed in his own sense of civilized superiority. The perceptive student, however, is confirmed in his conviction of the Bushman's intelligence. Kaow crumbles the dung, examines its texture, and smells it to see how far the poison has been assimilated into the animal's system, and to guess just how long he has to wait before it drops. In what the anthropologist Claude Lévi-Strauss calls "The Science of the Concrete,"[2] the mind of this savage is thinking concretely in terms of what we would more abstractly call the animal's mass, its metabolic rate, and the extrapolated time of death. It is the average student who is revolted by the sight of dung who is the real intellectual primitive, and, in fact, if he were to be trained as a doctor, he would have to learn to handle his data as dispassionately as Kaow.

Marshall's film is eloquent testimony in refutation of the still surviving belief in "the primitive mentality," but, more importantly, the film is also poetically eloquent in presenting in high relief the structure of a primary human group. As we follow Headman, Hunter, Clown, and Shaman, we can see that they perform as a set of complementary opposites. Using W. B. Yeats's model of psychological opposites, the structure of the group can be presented thus:

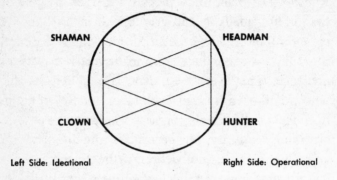

Left Side: Ideational   Right Side: Operational

PHASE I. THE TRIBAL COMMUNITY

The two triangles, taken from Yeats's *A Vision,*[3] are to be interpreted as two counterrotating gyres or tornadoes so fixed to one another that the narrowest point of one's power occurs at the maximum expansion of the other's. Since the sum of the angles of each equals 180 degrees, the sum of the two triangles equals the 360 degrees of the enclosing circle. The circle thus represents the unity of the field containing the two symmetrically opposed forces. The left gyre represents the Ideational; the right, the Operational. Headman and Hunter realize the possibilities that Shaman and Clown do not, as Shaman and Clown realize the possibilities untouched by the others. Together the four form a stable group in which all the skills are balanced. Although Kaow is the best hunter and the most physical of the four, they all must hunt and work together, so there is no extreme division of labor which can set the men apart from one another. The Headman must hunt with his men and his advice must be supported by strong reasons. He is no king on a throne. Since he is not enthroned, the Clown is only a part-time fool and a full-time hunter. And although the Hunter excels beyond the others, even the silent Shaman must hunt along with him. Because all share the same life, there is a generalized charisma in the group, and no institutional routines allow the Ideational and Operational modes to become violently opposed to one another. In tribal society the lack of a literate elite allows information to be shared equally through immediate sensory reading of the environment or through oral traditions. The four roles have clearly differentiated functions, but these functions are under the control of the strongly cohesive field of the tribal community.

This model of four seems to be a persistent one; it recalls the rule of four in the Indian caste system, Plato, Vico, Blake, Marx, Yeats, Jung, and McLuhan. So many people look out at reality and come up with a four-part structure that one cannot help but think that it expresses the nature of reality and/or the Kantian a priori pure categories of the understanding. But whether the structure exists in reality or is simply a projection of the categories of the human mind, is, of course, the traditionally unanswerable question of science. Since the mind is part of nature, we make a mistake when we imagine that the act of perception is through a window in which we are on one side and nature on the other. We are in nature, so there is no reason that subjectivity and objectivity should be so dissonantly arranged; it is more than likely that the key in which the nerves and the stars are strung is the same. But if the question is ultimately unknowable, we can be less ambitious by using the model as a heuristic device. If it helps us to see new things and explain some old things, then that should be enough.

PHASE II. AGRICULTURAL SOCIETY

The Tribal Society seems to express the value which Yeats called Unity of Being, for all the complementary and opposing forces seem to be in balance. But the appearance of an economic surplus created by the change from a food-gathering community to a food-producing society changes all that. The surplus enables society to support specialists, and this new specialization increases the distance between men in different roles. With the appearance of literate specialists, relations are no longer immediate but intermediate, for the new elite comes between man and the reading of his environment. An environment is a field of energy that supports the individual organism; information is the individual's means of storing energy and thereby controlling his relationship with the environment. Since information is a control of energy, a society is only as large as its capacity to store information. The grain stored in the Sumerian temple depended upon that urban society's ability to record and distribute that energy through the new informational system of cuneiform. Tribal man's memory is prodigious, but the amount of information an urban society can control is thousands of times greater. Yet individual man pays a price for this new collective achievement, for in many ways the move from individuals to institutions is a fall from unity to multiplicity. This urban transformation of the tribal community can be described in the following expansion of the original model, the germ plasm of civilization.

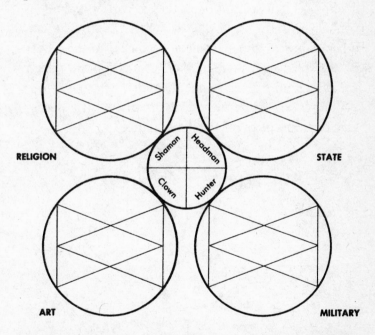

The economic surplus effects a social transformation whereby the part-time Shaman grows into the institution of Religion with its full-time specialists. The Headman grows into the institution of the State, the physical Hunter into the Military, and the Clown, who mocked the mysteries of the Shaman, the authority of the Headman, and the physical grace of the Hunter, into the institution of Art. Because men are now full-time specialists, they no longer have to share in one another's lives. Social distance becomes extreme as a new elite begins to lessen the authority of the other members of society. Now social roles become markedly differentiated and oppositions become more energetic as society tries to counteract the expanding forces of the new economy. Art is the opposite of the State; Religion is the opposite of the Military. Each institution activates certain values in conflict with its opposite, which seeks to activate other values. Human society becomes, in the terms of the physicist, a many-body situation in which *values can only be achieved in conflict with opposites.* This structural situation makes conflict itself a necessary function of organic differentiation.

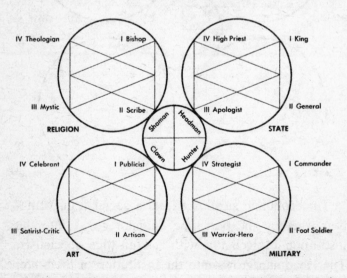

Left Side: Charismatic-Ideational   Right Side: Routine-Operational

PHASE II. AGRICULTURAL SOCIETY: FROM INDIVIDUALS TO INSTITUTIONS

But the expansion of urban society brings about a curious effect that tends to increase conflict and maintain stability at the same time. The original germ plasm of the primal four (Headman, Hunter, Clown, and Shaman) duplicates itself in every institution, and the loss of the generalized charisma of the tribal community now creates an opposition, in Max Weber's terms, between *routine* and *charisma* as well as between the operational and the ideational modes.

As an institution grows in complexity, it becomes impossible to have all the members of one mind. A religion of mystics would collapse as a social institution, and therefore what Weber calls "the routinization of charisma" allows the institution to employ its opposites within its own structure. This fall from unanimity to multiplicity is another expression of the philosophy implicit in the myth of original sin, for just as the conflict of opposites is inevitable, so it is inevitable that *every institution must subvert the values for which it was founded*. Every vision must be routinized to survive the death of the visionary, but every routinization of vision is only a bureaucratically disguised form of death, and so death is unavoidable. In the moral vision of the Hebrews, the condition is seen in terms of sin; in the cosmological vision of the Greeks, the condition is seen in terms of entropy, for all things must make reparation to the unlimited chaos from which they come, and to which they must, *of necessity,* return.

The duplication of the original four of the tribal community in every institution in urban society thus creates a field situation of simultaneous attraction and repulsion in which the Bishop administers the religion, the Scribe serves as the technician responsible for the important tool of writing, the Theologian relates the mythic tradition to the intellectual problems of society or the astronomical problems of the sacral calendar, and the Mystic dwells in the religious consciousness all the others, presumably, are striving to achieve. In pursuing his own task, each man must define himself in opposition to those on the other side of the circle, and relate himself in affinity with those who share his side. Astronomer and Mystic may differ, but they share a cosmic awareness that has little patience for the parochial point of view of Bishop and Scribe. Thus within the circle of an institution each member will attempt to expand the circle of his own power and influence until it is congruent with the entire circle. The Bishop thinks the Mystic is a foaming maniac; the Mystic thinks the Bishop is a callous money-grubber. The Scribe thinks the Theologian is a parasite upon his important work, and the Theologian thinks the Scribe is a mindless tool. In a stable institution the expansion of each will be checked by the mutual and complementary opposition of all. But this stability is affected by time, as Yeats points out in his more elaborate system, and so at various moments one role may be more powerful than the other three, thus throwing the institution out of classical Unity of Being.

This same process of duplication of the original four occurs in other institutions as well. Homer's *Iliad* presents a magnificent description of the conflict in values between the different roles in the Military. Agamemnon is the Commander; he is the routine-operational personality and sees the war in terms of the future plunder that is stored in Troy. His opposite is Achilles, the Hero, the man of divine gifts (charisma). For him the battle is a conflict with death in which his excellence is achieved as he blazingly vanishes into his destiny. He has nothing but contempt for the base Agamemnon. Crafty Odysseus is the Strategist. Once he tried to use his wiles in feigning madness to avoid serving under Agamemnon, and now he tries to end the war through trickery. His opposite is the trusty Ajax (the Foot Soldier), the plodding hulk who fights on with never a thought as to what it is all about.

In the institution of Art, the successful man in power would be someone like Phidias, the sculptor who was involved with Pericles in a scandal over the appropriations for the Parthenon. The opposite of this Publicist would be the Satirist-Critic, Aristophanes, the man who mocks the pretensions of those in power. Aeschylus would be a good example of the Celebrant, the man whose work celebrates the best of a civilization's tradition. His opposite is the practical Artisan, the man who does not set himself up as an institution, but simply plies his trade. Thus Publicist, Artisan, Satirist, and Celebrant in Art are perfect duplicates of Commander, Foot Soldier, Warrior, and Strategist in the Military.

In the institution of the State all the other institutions are coordinated. The King rules, but by his side are the General from the Military, the Apologist from Art, and the High Priest from Religion. By employing the routine-operational members of each institution in the governing structure, the rulers routinize the charisma of the opposing institutions and thus check the power of the divinely gifted but politically undependable men of the other side. Because people in similar structural positions are in affinity with one another, Establishments and Shadow Establishments develop. This can be seen in terms of the model if the four members are seen to inhabit the four quadrants of the circle. Thus those in quadrant one are in affinity with all other quadrant ones, and so on through all the quadrants and all the institutions. From this point of view there is nothing really so strange about a protest movement that embraces people as different as artists, warriors, and mystics; it is not a person's institution that determines his politics, but his role within his own institution.

The usefulness of this simplified Yeatsian model is that it enables us to see a few things about the nature of the conflict of values. Each person always thinks that he is right, but the model enables us to see that such a claim is the equivalent of an iron filing proclaiming that it is the total magnetic field. In terms of the total field, an individual cannot be a container of the truth; his action can only embody certain aspects of the truth. He can act out his role as superb tragedy or comedy, but he can never *be* the truth. The truth is what emerges in the field of the sphere as one man engages his opposite in conflict. This is precisely Yeats's very Greek tragic vision, and is what he saw shortly before he died when he wrote to a friend that man could never know the truth, he could only embody it so the truth could be seen in him by someone, God or Daimon, looking at history from the outside.

This field condition of values thus presents us with a relativism in the context of a universal absolute. If we stand furiously in our personalities in the theater of conflict of history, our actions can only be tragic or comic, appropriate or inappropriate. If we stand in our daimonic consciousness outside of history, we become full of truth because we can hold onto no thing. But man lives at the place where time and eternity meet, and that is a place of crucifixion where the opposites cross. In the human world of conflict, every action creates its equal and opposite reaction, and so static values can only be mocked by the very dynamic process of history itself.

With the growth of urban civilization, man loses the old community of the tribe, and so a reaction occurs and nativistic revolts attempt to restore man to the hallowed ways of his pastoral ancestors and gods. As we see pastoral prophet and urban priest clash all through the pages of the Old Testament, we observe, safely from the outside, a tragedy in which each man requires the other. Judaism was a tribal religion, not an urban one, but the only way the tribes could protect themselves from the threat of the more advanced urban Canaanites was *to become like them through conflict with them*. So by the time of King Solomon, the Jews were wealthy urban Canaanites and a new poverty separated rich Jew from poor Jew in ways that Father Abraham would have abhorred. The prophets arise and attack the new society of palaces and temples, but an unheeding arrogance precedes Israel's fall. However, centuries later when the Jews return from the concentration camps of Babylon, it is not to become pastoral again. For Amos, the shepherd, an urban Jew is a contradiction in terms, but after the suffering in Babylon the holy *city* of Jerusalem becomes a reality in ways which were not possible for the wealthy Jerusalem of King Solomon. After the urbanization of King David, and the pastoral revitalization of Amos, a new synthesis is achieved and a Jew can still be a Jew and live in a city. Like the *Iliad,* the Old Testament is a great work of art that shows how Jahweh (like Zeus) works *through* a universe of conflict in which David, who builds the city, and Amos, who attacks it (like Achilles, who attacks the city, and Hector, who defends it), can both be simultaneously magnificent (and right) and wrong.

History is thus inescapably a tragedy in which man may choose between forms of tyrnanny but never can escape the tyranny of form. Man is formed by the universe in which he moves, and in the world of multiplicity of men and atoms, all things are colliding and rushing toward entropy. When man fell from unity into multiplicity, he moved into a world in which he could only realize himself in conflict with his opposite in the contradictions of time. The archetypal Adam and Eve are the first set of conflicting opposites, which announce in microcosm all the conflicting opposites to come. Now in the broken world of politics, the enemy, like the lover, is the complement to a fragmented being. The historical recapitulation of the myth of original sin is seen in the fall from the unity and generalized charisma of the tribal community into the multiplicity and routines of civilized man. With culture polarized between charisma and routine, Shaman and Priest fight in ways that would shock both the Headman and Shaman of the tribal order.

The liberal optimist would like to pretend that conflict is merely an aberration, a temporary dysfunction of an unenlightened behavioral system, and that once we have either the ultimate revolution or the advice of behavioral engineers, we will have peace, truth, and goodness forever. But to claim this he first blinds himself in an ignorance of history in which behavior is isolated from all the factors that give it meaning, and then claims that the factors he carefully eliminated never existed in the first place. Achilles, too, tried to change the universe and ignore the myth of original sin, and in the funeral games for Patroclus he tried to set up a new mircocosm (like B. F. Skinner's *Walden Two*) in which evil and conflict were expelled by a new order in which the winner, the runner-up, and the loser all took prizes. But the contestants in the games asserted themselves, just as atoms do in the cosmos, and came into conflict. The only way Achilles could secure his new peaceful world was by interfering with it at every moment of its existence. He, too, had to enter the theater of conflict to stop the inevitable conflicts. But Achilles was a tragic hero and not a social scientist; he saw his error and no longer tried to escape destiny, but went out to meet his fate with all the excellence of his role as warrior.

When a man realizes his destiny, he is only seeing his own tragic historical role from the mythical perspective of the whole field. He can seek to escape his destiny and avoid all action whatsoever, knowing that it doesn't matter, for his enemy is right in a

way, even if he does block his own way; or he can
act with the religious detachment of Karma Yoga
that Krishna explained to Arjuna. When a man ac-
cepts the tragedy and goes forth to action, as Faulkner says, "knowing better," he begins to be more
of a mythical creature than a historical being. Whether
it is a Gandhi sustained by God or a Mao sustained
by the dialectics of history, the mythical creature is
a hero whose proportions are frighteningly larger
for the rest of us who cower in the chorus.

But the tragedy is even more complex than that.
Because an individual cannot contain the truth, it
means that only the ignorant claim to be free. The
wise understand exactly what a world weighs down
upon them. And so we have a paradox: the ignorant
scream that they are free of the tragedy, and in
claiming to be liberated individuals can never truly
be so. The wise know that the individual is not and
cannot be free, and, therefore, in expressing the will
of God or the Marxist dialectics of history, they become free. He who would gain his life must lose it.
And that is an older attack on "bourgeois personalism" than the one invented by SDS. The young
individual forces himself to believe that only his
action is right, that all others are wrong. But when
he begins to see the possibility that his enemy completes him more profoundly than his "groupies,"
he is forced into the recognition that he must cherish
his enemy. What most regard as a Christian plati-
tude is, in reality, a rather sophisticated attempt to
reverse the tragedy of conflict.

Let me make this anarchism as clear as possible
by being as apodictic as possible: no political sys-

tem can work because no political system can escape the structural contradictions inherent in the necessity of achieving values in a system which subverts the values themselves. No merely historical process can work for the individual or society, because no historical process can escape the structural contradictions of history. The technocrat merely builds his castles of sand in summer at the edge of a seasonally raging sea on which he has turned his back. If all things are rushing toward entropy, pure anarchism only accelerates the process by claiming man is inherently free. Inverse entropy, the *conservation* of value in a world of chaos, comes from a religious transformation in which a disadvantage on one level of order becomes an advantage on a higher level of order. Every creation is preceded by the right kind of chaos needed for a universe. From a civilized point of view the lack of bureaucracies (churches and universities) is a disadvantage, but from the Zen or Yoga anarchic point of view individuals, and not institutions, are the only things that can be filled with value. When the individual walks out of a bureaucracy (education: *ex ducere:* to lead out), he becomes empty enough to be filled with *samadhi* or *satori*. Then, and only then, is the fall reversed; then and only then is he inherently free. He is free to return. In the words of the Zen koan: "First there is a mountain, then there is no mountain, then there is."

The individual's consciousness in meditation takes him out of history; it gives him a glimpse of the total field beyond his personal location. At first this glimpse is destructive of identity, but when the person finds that he survives the loss of his ego, he realizes that

there is more to his identity, and he begins to see
that just as there is more to him, there is more to
history than politics. Politics is to civilization what
the ego is to the self. When the individual glimpses
this larger vision, he is free, like Arjuna, to return
with an expanded consciousness of the totality realizing itself through the many-body system of oppositions. If education could lead all men out of the
bureaucracies of churches and universities into the
consciousness that comes from meditation, then conflict could be lifted up into a ritual-game and war
would be unnecessary: or would it be, as the conservatives and liberals might say, only that war
would no longer be so frightening?

At whatever level we choose to look at it, the
tragedy of conflict will undoubtedly continue, for even
out of history the individual is forced to see that he
is not all one thing, and that those other things
against which he rages have their equivalents within
him. The model of the community becomes, therefore, the correspondent model of the self.

Blakes fourfold vision becomes threefold in soft
Beulah's night, and so it does in Freud's eyes as
well. Daimon, Self, and Creative Mind are elimi-

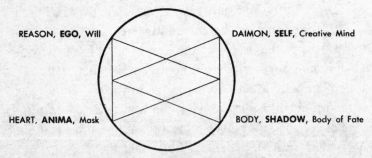

REASON, **EGO**, Will   DAIMON, **SELF**, Creative Mind

HEART, **ANIMA**, Mask   BODY, **SHADOW**, Body of Fate

THE FOUR PARTS OF THE SELF: PLATO, **JUNG**, AND Yeats

nated, and we end up with the three of Superego, Ego, and Id. It is the nineteenth-century *haut bourgeois* vision: authority has decayed into the authoritarian father who inflicts upon the children the ancient myths he no longer understands. Naturally, for those children there can be no Daimon recognized in the self, or in the civilization at large, for there is always just that correspondence between self and society. As Sorokin has observed: "The individual has as many different social egos as there are different social groups and strata with which he is connected."[4] A pluralistic society breaks up the self; its many institutions hold out conflicting and contradictory roles, and when an individual who must play separate roles as he moves from institution to institution encounters a contradiction between the instructions for one role and the values expressed in the traditional myths, he experiences the stress of "cognitive dissonance." The very social structures or routines that are created to preserve values become the walls and corridors that break up the mythic landscape into the cubicle-empires of a thousand authoritarian bureaucrats. The movement from tribal community to agricultural society is thus a dazzling leap up to civilization, and a dramatic fall from unity into fragmentation.

PHASE III. INDUSTRIAL CIVILIZATION

Now that we have been speaking of thousands of years it is time to sharpen our focus to speak merely of centuries. The Protestant ethic and the spirit of capitalism encouraged work and prosperity, as Weber has pointed out, but it also encouraged the democratization of information through the printed Bible, as McLuhan has pointed out. Cromwell's middle classes manned the crafts, while the scientific elite, with Newton, hid from them but still provided the seventeenth-century physics that would be necessary for eighteenth-century mechanization. Thousands of years stretch between hunting society and agricultural society, and thousands of years stretch between agricultural society and industrial society. It remains to be seen if our military and industrial technology will permit thousands of years to stretch between industrial society and scientific civilization.

When we consider the third stage of industrial civilization more closely, we can see that the former agricultural movement from individuals to institutions now expands from institutions to corporate systems. The chief feature of agricultural civilization was its ability to store information far beyond the limits of tribal society. Industry runs on paper as much as on coal, and if English mercantile society had had no means of producing and controlling the vast amounts of information commerce generated, the Industrial Revolution would never have happened. When one regards cultures as systems of information as well as production, then there is no reason why Marx, Weber, and McLuhan cannot be employed simultaneously in a historical description that recognizes that economics and ideology affect one another in a reciprocal causal alternation. The model for industrial civilization, expanded from its previous feudal state, would thus look like this:

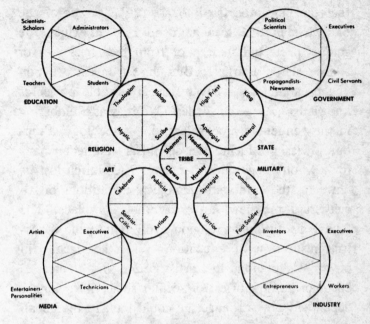

PHASE III. INDUSTRIAL CIVILIZATION: FROM INSTITUTIONS TO CORPORATE SYSTEMS

The Industrial Revolution in eighteenth-century England began a process that has only now completed itself in North America. What most people refer to as "postindustrial" society is really only industrial society at last free of the restraints of feudal institutions. The entrepreneurial capitalism of rugged individualism has been replaced by a managerial society of executives, but, as McLuhan has pointed out, "The principle that during the stages of their development all things appear under forms opposite to those that they finally present in an ancient doctrine."[5] In 1760 the capitalist found places to grow in that were not covered by feudal institutions, but by 1795 his growth began to push against those institutions so that the landlords tried to assert the power of the old ways in the Speenhamland Law in which the squires protected their poor from the necessities of a free labor market.[6] But the strongest weapon of the capitalist was always the irresistible power of knowledge. At a time when Oxford was slumbering in the gentlemanly consideration of theology, Edinburgh was producing the scientists and technicians for a wholly new kind of society. The church lost its power as the dominant ideological institutions of society and the new university took its place. The feudal institution of religion evolved into the industrial institution of education. With the decline in power of religion, the artist seized his chance to become the new priest of secular society. No longer dependent on patronage, he could look to the cheap mass production of books to provide him with an independent income. Free of lords and prelates, he could even become an institution with his own public: e.g., Dickens and the lending libraries.

On the operational side of industrial society, the expansion of business broke the power of the old landowning elite, and the introduction of all the middle-class technicians transformed the state (*"L'état, c'est moi?"*) into government. And with the rise of capitalism, the military was no longer the aristocratic horseman, but the whole industrial capacity. A great industrial capacity makes a great war possible, which in turn increases the industrial capacity. The expanding industrial capacity requires new forms of efficiency and rationalization of human habits. Unfortunately, the new efficiency threatens the old organic Unity of Being through differentiation. Religion, Art, the Military, and the State were settled into traditional ways of opposing one another in feudal agricultural civilization, but with the rapid transformation brought on by the Industrial Revolution, there was a general panic as all the institutions rushed to find their positions in the expanding structure.

In a society of corporate systems, on Marx's terms, the alienation of the individual is extreme. The chance for charismatic influence is greatly reduced because a floating elite of routine-operational managers circulates through government, industry, education, and the media to give them a single character. The triumph of the routine operational mentality thus destroys the chance for Unity of Being through differentiation. Education is the first to suffer, for the university is the central nervous system of the complex. The fall of prophetic vision into departments of religion turns the old feudal institution into a new apologist for liberal, technocratic ambitions: witness the writings of Harvey Cox.[7] The poet becomes the professor of creative writing and an apologist for the routinization of literature's former charisma. In the universities the liberals are offering Richard Wilbur as an example of the modern poet, but the media are fighting the corporate system by lifting up the old individual. The artist undergoes a sea-change and surfaces as Bob Dylan or the Beatles. And in the case when the old artists sense the movement from solitary Tolstoy or Gaugin to mass-media personality, we have Norman Mailer and Andy Warhol. Industrial society thus produces the system of communication which the charismatic personalities use to subvert industrial society, much in the same way that Roman engineers built the roads that Christian missionaries traveled to convert an empire.

The media, of course, should not be seen as a totally charismatic institution. They, too, are dominated by routine-operational minds and try, through the news, to serve as an institution of business and government. The routine-operational men in the media gather with the routine-operational men in education and industry to form the Establishment. But it is not only those in the first quadrant who line up with their corresponding types in the other corporate systems; all the quadrants align themselves in affinity with their corresponding quadrants, and this alignment of Establishment and the protesting Shadow Establishment has a curious effect on the social structure. On the one hand, it helps to check the power of the government by creating powerful new associations, but since the government plays that game as well, the new alignments across the lines of conflict only make the field situation more dynamic.

The ideational intellectuals are scientific and technological, so although they are on the side of charisma, they cannot share with those in the third quadrant their nativistic attack on technology. This causes the intellectuals in the fourth quadrant to reach across to the first to serve as advisers to the government. Some of the most charismatic of the scientists spurn their bureaucratic colleagues to associate with an oppositional group of artists, scientists, Nobel laureates, and students; but enough of the intellectuals are coopted that the organic differentiation is threatened by routine-operational sameness in all corporate systems. But just as many scientists in the fourth quadrant cooperate with the gigantic government, so many nativist students cooperate with the lower-middle-class Far Right in its attack on the liberal technostructure. The model for the present state of conflict would look like this:

Left Side: Charismatic-Ideational   Right Side: Routine-Operational

CONTEMPORARY SOCIETY

The four quadrants are distinctly opposed to one another, but at the interfaces between opposing quadrants there are ideological sharings which simultaneously create forms of social stability and forms of social change. Because the conservatives and liberals affirm the value of our technological culture, they create a stable situation in which the liberal technocrats in the universities are associated with the industrialists in the government. But the very fact that the liberals live in the universities exposes them to the new nonindustrial, informational culture. People who work in the media or the professions are more visibly hip than the industrial conservatives.

They are modly attired and they engage in T groups and the whole Esalen Institute range of behavior. Many of them smoke marijuana, and so they share the hip culture of the radicals.

Industrial culture stresses sobriety, paternal wisdom, caution, thrift, and the postponement of sensuous gratification in order to achieve long-term financial prosperity—all amounting to the familiar work ethic. Informational culture stresses joy, youthful spontanenity, energy, abandon, and the postponement of financial security in order to achieve immediate sensuous self-realization. Industrial culture is one of sexual repression, which finds its outlet in the power of mechanization. In the case of the wealthy industrialist, this power is sublimated into the acceptable forms of a man who dominates factories and financial empires. In the case of a member of the industrial working class, the power is seen in his car, motorcycle, or, in Vietnam, his gunmanship— witness the air pilot who was incensed that "one of the little mothers was firing at us" and met the situation with an appropirate technological response. Informational culture is one of sexual expression in the complete body, which sublimates physical aggression into a form of erotic provocation of those who appear to be sexually repressed.

Industrial and informational cultures met head on at the Democratic National Convention in Chicago in 1968 and the result is history. The members of informational culture attacked through Eros, and the members of industrial culture attacked through Thanatos. The liberated young girls in miniskirts and no-bra T-shirts shouted "fuck" to the police, and thereby mocked their lower-class station in which women were not permitted to swear, and made fun of their dumb-cop Irish-Catholic background. Enfolded in the arms of long-haired boys, the girls would approach the line of National Guard troops and softly ask: "Wouldn't you rather hold me than that gun?" In this form of class war, a college girl made fun of a lower-middle-class man who could never expect to pal around with her kind. The power of sex overcame the radicals' smallness in numbers, and the erotically provoked police exploded into a riot. Out came the phallic clubs, and the miniskirts were left, according to the photographs in *Life,* falling in the opposite direction on the deliberately rough-handled girls. The industrial class had attacked the informational class before in the Century City police riot of 1967 in Los Angeles, but never before had the bitter gulf between the opposite ends of the great American middle class been so clearly marked as in this mythopoeic battle between Eros and Thanatos—a battle that recalls the closing lines of Freud's *Civilization and Its Discontents*:

The fateful question for the human species seems to me to be whether and to what extent their cultural development will succeed in mastering the disturbance of their communal life by the human instinct of aggression and self-destruction. It may be that in this respect precisely the present time deserves a special interest. Men have gained control over the forces of nature to such an extent that with their help they would have no difficulty in exterminating one another to the last man. They know this, and hence comes a large part of their current unrest, their unhappiness and their mood of anxiety. And now it is to be expected that the other of the two "Heavenly Powers," eternal Eros, will make an effort to assert himself in the struggle with his equally immortal adversary. But who can foresee with what success and with what result?[8]

The oppositions in conflict are always fierce, but what makes conflict more complicated than a simple black-and-white condition is that *in the circle one quadrant belongs simultaneously to two different halves.* At one interface of the fourth quadrant the liberals are attached to the conservatives in government; at the other they are attached to the radical culture of the students. And so it is with the radicals. At the interface with the liberals they share educational values and are working in traditional terms for advanced degrees. But at the other interface of the third quadrant, the radicals reject liberal values and share with the reactionaries the political belief in the necessity of force. Together these radicals and reactionaries share a contempt for the bureaucratic liberal technostructure. This doubled system of sharing in ideologies creates a situation in which the radical sector is stabilized by being aligned with the Establishment liberals and revolutionized by being aligned with the reactionaries who negate moderation and affirm extremist violence. Thus the radical Left and the radical Right, as has often been noticed before, are next to one another, as the circle indicates. The actions of the radicals feed the reactionaries, witness Ronald Reagan and Berkeley, and without their confrontation politics the radical Right would starve for lack of a conspiracy. The more the radicals and reactionaries interact with one another, the more difficult it becomes for the liberals and conservatives to rule in moderation. The reactionaries farthest away from power share the violent rhetoric of the radicals and hope to see a complete reversal of the liberal technostructure through extreme social reaction. And so the radicals and reactionaries are lovers in disguise, and in the streets of Chicago, 1968, each received gratification beyond his wildest hopes.

The reactionaries closer to the ruling moderates, however, share their industrial culture and are attired in the ceremonial robes of business and free enterprise. They do not want a reversal of the liberal technostructure because they have it successfully under control in the military-industrial complex. On one side the reactionaries are aligned with the radicals (and hope that SDS will burn a university to the ground so that they can come to power in 1972 on their own terms and not on the coattails of the conservatives), and on the other side they are aligned with the moderates. And so it is with the conservatives themselves, for they can reach across into the liberal quadrant to take Kissinger from Harvard and Moynihan from M.I.T., while maintaining Attorney General Mitchell, J. Edgar Hoover, and Richard Kleindienst.

Now if we look at this wheel of ideological positions and ask ourselves who is right and who is wrong, we will see that all the positions are simultaneously wrong and right. The reactionaries are practically fascists, but they are also the radical conservators of the traditions of preindustrial America, and thus they are the violent opponents of the ruling bureaucracy of experts who would tell them how to

educate their children according to the best advice
of the Office of Education. The opposites of the
reactionaries are thus, as liberals, the naïve conduc-
tors to the Brave New World. But, on the other hand,
the right to raise your own children means creating
the freedom and space in which to educate them to
hate education, Negroes, and foreigners, and to love
the Ku Klux Klan. The situation reverses itself, and
now the spineless and unprincipled bureaucrat from
Washington is seen as a champion of human rights.
The difficulty is that we cannot achieve liberal values
collectively without creating the social structural situation that activates liberal vices. And the condition
is the same for the reactionaries: we cannot achieve
the rural values of the past without creating the space
for George Wallace to grow in. We are thus in a
condition of "double-bind," the fallen human condition mythically described as original sin. The radicals
are a force for good and social change, and because
they have no power, they do not sell out. But precisely because they have no power they irresponsibly
wish to destroy all structures and look upon a troop-
controlled university as an honest picture of the real
America.

If we switch across the wheel to escape the evils
of reactionaries, radicals, and liberals, we encounter
conservatives who wish to conserve nothing more
than the military-industrial system. But we also see
a stable force of routine-operational minds that keeps
society from breaking down into anarchy. Anarchy
for the radicals is a vision of liberation in which students can play in a "People's Park" without being
sprayed with vomit gas by helicopters, but real an-

archy is one in which there is no food in the super-
markets, no water in the faucets, no electric power,
no ambulances, and no police protection from roam-
ing bandits except for the Right-minded friends of
the reactionary police. *And so there is no position
on the wheel that expresses the truth.*

The liberals are for reason and free speech; they
are also for social engineering and the adjustment of
the individual to the technological society through
the aid of behavioral therapy. Their vision is of a
cosmic void ennobled by the presence of so many
liberal Ph.D.'s. When one joins the liberals, he discovers that he has assented to more than he wishes.
If he tries to assert his own peculiar combination of
opposites, he finds himself without the association.
Nevertheless, his tenuous association with the liberals is enough to alienate the radicals. If he goes
over with the radicals, he finds a politics of emotion
which is a warm human antidote to behavioral engineering and an antidote to reason as well. A stay
with the radicals, with their masochistic lust for punishment, is likely to set him thinking in terms of
Burke's and Blake's criticism of tyrants and rebels.
If he moves over to the conservatives, he finds people
who are uninterested in Burke or Blake, but very
interested in the empire of capitalism. The conservatives turn out to be little different from the Establishment liberals of the new technocracy.

If this encounter sets him in to a rage against
cabals and elites and into fantasies of yeoman America, he will find that the good common people are
yelling against miscegenation and screaming for capital punishment and force as resolutions of all

problems, foreign and domestic. Looking at the civilization expressed in the wheel, we see a tragedy in which the artistically uncompromising vision of the poet has demanded that his art transcend his mere opinions; each character is to be presented as simultaneously right and wrong so that the truth will be expressed, not in the characters, but in the epic. And that is the timeless Homeric vision.

The Homeric vision of love and death in human nature has persisted throughout 2,700 years of history, but we are now at a new threshold in cultural evolution in which that human nature itself may be tampered with. The new biological technology is beginning to give some men the power to alter basic human nature in order to achieve, beyond love and death, the rational society.[9] The Homo Sapiens of Eros and Thanatos may be coming to an end, and Homo Sapiens seem unconsciously aware of this, but this terrified awareness only generates an apocalyptic hysteria which in turn convinces the behavioral engineers that rationality cannot be achieved without fixing man. The elimination of familial sexuality in procreation and the licensing of child-bearing by the state should go a long way in taming still savage man and making him fit for a technological civilization, or so the technicians will reason.

If that biological transformation isn't enough to contend with, we must also face the fact that the informational explosion is straining human rationality to the breaking point. Rationality was possible in Greek, Roman, and European civilizations because there were only a few hundred books one needed to know. We have now reached the point where even an academic who devotes his whole life to reading cannot possibly keep up, even with his own limited field. If one is spending all his time reading in his own field to maintain his expertise, he is not reading the books in related fields that may be even more important for his work than the material in his own professional journals. If one is trying to keep up with science or scholarship, he cannot keep up with society or be a parent to children; which is only to say that the family and bourgeois democracy are dying along with print, Homo Sapiens, and the industrial nation-state. We have reached the end of what we have known as civilization and we do not need bombs to destroy it.[10]

The young feel intuitively what is happening, and that is why we are witnessing the forms of revolt and withdrawal around us. When rationality is not possible because the institution of reason, the university, overloads the mind with data without meaning, the institution perishes in its own excremental productivity. Once the individual is without the institution, he can ascend to suprarational levels of imagination, intuition, and creativity or descend to the levels of subrational panic. This rejection of rationality can be clearly seen in the remarks of one SDS leader, Eric Mann:

> You'd better be committed to the idea that reality is found in books, because the whole university system revolves around that concept. If you like to sing, if you like to organize, you can do that. But it's called extra-curricular. . . . Now to start with, I think a lot of us wouldn't want to be here, if that was the definition of four years of our life.[11]

Eric Mann, Jerry Rubin, Abbie Hoffman—these are the members of my generation who were raised upon the social sciences of the postwar multiversity. And now they have discovered that they are neither social nor scientific, and in a rage against their own stupidity for ever having been made fools of, they have gleefully adopted the fool's ceremonial robes and phallic wand. They have tried to find a place for human nature in the rationalized, technological society, but the only place that is left for human nature is in the office of the fool. To air-conditioned canisters of glass and steel, they bring their own sacrificial folly. The body and the emotions are their weapons; rationality is their enemy, and in the conflict of the one against the other, our whole society is coming to pieces. Now as the whole thing totters and sways back and forth, it seems that there are only two sides to which it can fall.

If Berkeley has proven the weakness of liberal humanism with its belief that public education would bring salvation, then, the radicals argue, we have only our passionate bodies to fall back upon. But it is very clear now as we watch this play between the expressions of Eros and the repressions of Thanatos that the whole passionate drama is only playing into the dispassionate hands of the behavioral engineers. When Eros and Thanatos have exhausted themselves, Logos and Agapé will return. The sophisticated guardians will appear, to rescue us from the violent passions of extreme Left and Right, with a new human administration, for positive reinforcement is only another name for love.[12] No longer will we need the terror of the seventies, for by the time of the eighties "The Invisible College" will surface out of the darkness of the American Cromwellian Protectorate to offer a new, *refined* vision of the technological millennnium. Protest to the new triumph of Logos will, of course, arise, but the protest can only be futile; the age of protest, of violent demonstrations, will have passed. As the Indians were to the technology of the railroads in the nineteenth century, so now are the unscientific human beings to the new technology of behavioral engineering. But if the ancient doctrine that things in their development appear in a form opposite to those they finally present is still true, then perhaps the tyranny of Logos will finally give us the forms in which to achieve the miracle of Agapé. As de Chardin has said:

Every new war, embarked upon by the nations for the purpose of detaching themselves from one another, merely results in their being bound and mingled together in a more inextricable knot. The more we seek to thrust each other away, the more do we interpenetrate. . . . The last day of Man will coincide for Mankind with the maximum of its tightening and in-folding upon itself.

. . . Although our individualistic instincts may rebel against this drive toward the collective, they do so in vain and wrongly. In vain, because no power in the world can enable us to escape from what is in itself the power of the world. And wrongly because the real nature of this impulse ["the planetisation of mankind"] that is sweeping us towards a state of super-organization is such as to make us more completely personalized and human.

The very fact of becoming aware of this profound

ordering of things will enable human collectivisation to pass beyond the *enforced* phase, where it is now, into the *free* phase.[13]

From this dizzyingly high mystical perspective, the Devil, at the end of history, takes off his mask and proves to be Christ in disguise. The behavioral engineers, who collectivized mankind in order to control it efficiently, ironically create the planetary media through which the planetization of mankind is effected. It is a variation of the old story in which Caesar calls for an administrative census that brings Christ into the City of David. There is a profound recognition of the dialectical nature of history in de Chardin's vision, for it is quite obvious now that television has had some radical political effects that were not planned by the engineers of RCA and Zenith, but the great difficulty with the visions of such Catholic thinkers as Teilhard de Chardin, Marshall McLuhan and Ivan Illich[14] is that they can serve as apologies for collectivization. If we have come to the end of "the Protestant Ethic and the Spirit of Capitalism," as these Catholic thinkers naturally want to believe, then we have come to the end of the age of print (McLuhan), the end of the age of universal public education (Illich), and the end of the middle-class democracies with their industrial nation-states (de Chardin). We eliminate the middle to achieve a new energized top and bottom: scientists and hippies, Pythagoreans and superstitious techno-peasants. No doubt the new medievalism, like the old, will be both angelic and demonic at once. Short of the hippies' expected return of the gods in their flying saucers, or the Second Coming of Christ, the tragedy of history will continue, and the double-bind condition of human nature will remain.

Unfortunately, we don't seem to have any choice. The defense of the nation-state now threatens the planet; the Gross National Product has created a new ecological consciousness of nature. The union of science and nationalism controlled by secret police is coming to an end. With smaller nations developing a nuclear capacity, and with the American government firmly in the hands of the reactionary military technologists, it is becoming clear to the pure scientists that if the planet's knowledge were invested in a close, international fraternity, that fraternity would be stronger than the nation-state. As one disaster after another hits the earth between now and the year 2000, it will be possible for the scientists to effect a palace coup in the planet. In a state of panic and exhaustion brought on by the disasters, the people will have no other alternative but to look up to their saviors who can promise to keep the life-support systems of Space Ship Earth working—at the price of absolute scientific control over environments and populations. If world famine, overpopulation, pollution, ecological catastrophes, and the patriotic use of nuclear weapons bring us to another Dark Age, then obviously another ecclesiastical structure will arise from the ashes of the old order.

But what went on before over centuries will then take only decades. Now man is free of myth and complains of alienation and a loss of purpose; then all men will be together in the culture of suffering and will share a high sense of purpose, but man will not be free in the ways we know him to be free today.

If the disasters do not simply end civilization altogether, then some form of scientific-planetary civilization will succeed the industrial civilization of the
nation-state. If there is anything beyond the year
2000, then Phase IV will not be Chaos, with Phase
V as the Tribal Phase I all over again, but will look
something like this:

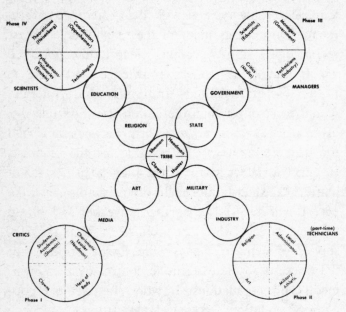

PHASE IV. SCIENTIFIC-PLANETARY CIVILIZATION: THE INDIVIDUAL AS INSTITUTION

PHASE IV. SCIENTIFIC-PLANETARY
CIVILIZATION

Phase III (Industrial Civilization) of the foregoing
model expresses maximum alienation and fragmentation in contrast with tribal society. The ethos of
civilization has broken down entirely in the shift from

institutions to corporate systems, and operational routines take the place of myth and systems of belief. Rather than expressing the differentiation of an organic system, all four quadrants express the triumph of the routine-operational mentality, for there are no essential differences among big government, big industry, big education, and big media. But, as often happens in history, the widest point of one gyre is the beginning point of another; the apex is the beginning of the decline. Media destroy the sacrosanct quality of novel and poem and replace James Joyce and Dylan Thomas with Jean-Luc Godard and Bob Dylan. But the decentralization made possible by the informational revolution also makes concentrations unnecessary. One does not have to pay the heavy price of living in New York just to be close to things. One does not have to be at Berkeley if the campus at Santa Cruz has information-retrieval systems and videophones that permit intercampus consultations.

McLuhan has remarked that the effect of the electronic informational explosion is to make possible a new nonverbal cosmic consciousness; but it is more likely to be a new cosmic unconsciousness. In the elimination of language there is implicit in this cultural transformation the growth of a very undemocratic Pythagorean brotherhood. When information is so immense that man cannot keep up with it and still be purely rational, he has a choice: he can freak out and become tribal again to attack the old naïve rational values in the guise of a Luddite-student; or he can effect a quantum leap in consciousness to re-vision the universe. Those who have effected the shift to cosmic consciousness will probably serve as future versions of the Athenian elect who were initiate to the mysteries.

For those who cannot re-vision the universe in the mystical, mathematical, and scientific forms of the new Pythagoreanism, there will be other forms of association. Since the new often miniaturizes the old according to McLuhan's formula, the part-time technicians of automated society will probably internalize Phase II. They will be, as many already are now, deacons or ministers of churches, officers in antique armies, and leaders of local communities. In each case the technicians will be practitioners of the *old* form of religion, the military, art, and government. In an age of the new paganism, they will be the old churchgoers; in an age of neutron rays, they will be captains of rifle squads; in an age of immaterial art, they will be sculptors of matter in the fashion of Rodin or viola da gambists; in an age of world government, they will run the towns and small cities with which human history began. This antiquarianism should not be looked upon with undue scorn, for it is one very valuable way in which mankind maintains the value of the old in face of the upheavals of the new.

Phase IV is simply Phase I on a planetary scale. It is the new myth which spins the Viconian cycle over again, or it is the retribalized Global Village in McLuhan's terms. The serpent bites its tail, and we spiral up to another plane by moving back into a correspondence of the old. A new cosmic myth succeeds the linear fragmentation of Phase III, and man once again confronts the universe with his body, mind, and soul to see that his petty industrial technology of Phase III was a very tiny thing indeed. In the new myth, Manager, Technician, Critic, and Scientist are what, in the old order, were Headman, Hunter, Clown, and Shaman.

In Scientific-Planetary Civilization the humanist is the clown. He does not speak the sacred language of mathematics and is not initiate to the mysteries. We can see this development growing already, for the Yippies are not the future mathematicians of our age; they are the old liberal arts majors who are smart enough to see that being an English major and getting a Ph.D. is a very irrelevant and unfulfilling act in our apocalyptic era. And just as long ago the Clown mocked the authority of the Headman, and the beauty of the Hunter, and the seriousness of the Shaman, so now the Critics of Scientific Civilization mock the authority of the Managers, the productivity of the Technicians, and the disembodied chimeras of the Theoreticians.

The Critics are the complementary opposites of the Managers; they are the jesters with donkey ears and cap and bells, phallic wand, and antic dance. Together all the Critics miniaturize Phase I, for in the last phase the model completes itself. Just as in Phase II the original four of the tribal phase duplicated themselves in every institution, so now each phase of history duplicates itself in the quadrants. The Critics are Phase I, the Technicians are Phase II, the Managers are Phase III, and the ultimate Scientists are Phase IV.

With special reference to the sphere of the Critics, the Headman is in the first quadrant. He is a charismatic leader rather than a political scientist: a Malcolm X. In the second quadrant is the Hero of the Body, like Kaow the Beautiful in *The Hunters*. Since the body is the romantic landscape of the scientific age, sexuality and physical mysticism (like Yoga) will play an important part in asserting man's distinctness from his civilized surroundings. In the terms of Robert Heinlein's popular science fiction novel, *Stranger in a Strange Land,* Michael Valentine Smith and his religion of sexuality represent the kind of nativism a Scientific Civilization would likely contain. In the third quadrant of the Critical sphere is the Clown. The Clown gives the cry of the heart against necessity and plays Pierrot to the body's Columbine. Bob Dylan, Jerry Rubin, and, in a middle-aged way, Norman Mailer demonstrate that the clowns of our present Technological Society are the entertainers, the artists, and the personalities. This magnification of the personality is one compensatory feature of mass society, for the media that are responsible for the destruction of the individual are also responsible for a movement away from corporate systems to the individual as institution. This, too, is a miniaturization of the old order, for the new psychic forms of art, religion, and politics make the individual seem merely a cell in a larger organism. But the compensatory feature of the individual as institution is beautiful while it lasts.

In terms of our present drift toward this state, we can see that in the academic profession the professor is moving away from being a professor of some one thing in a department (the worst aspects of Phase III) and is becoming simply a thinker in an environment of tools (the old disciplines) provided by a university wishing to have him as camouflage for its routine bureaucratic functions. The University of Toronto's Center for Culture and Technology is simply Marshall McLuhan; the University of Southern Illinois is Buckminster Fuller. The patronage of the university, however, will be probably short-lived, and the centers and institutes will have to move their Pythagorean mysteries off campus. Just as once the ecclesiastic hierarchy went into eclipse as the charisma of society shifted from the church to the university, so, no doubt, will the academic hierarchy go into eclipse as the charisma shifts to the smaller, more elect Ionas and Lindisfarnes.

In the fourth quadrant of the Critical sphere are the intellectuals who, for all their intelligence, cannot speak the sacred language of number. These will be the students and academics, who follow with great interest, criticize, but cannot take part in the world of science, music, and mathematics. They will be like the old pagans watching Christianity take over Europe. Their function will be to create a consciousness of human civilization; since they stand at a distance from science, they see the things the scientists cannot. Like Hephaestus, the cripple, who made the beautiful armor for all the beautiful bodies of the gods and heroes, the humanist succeeds because he is a failure.

Opposite to the sphere of the humanistic Critics is the sphere of the planetary Managers. These will be the administrators of all the institutions, but they are slightly more human in the twenty-first century. The disasters of the declining twentieth century have tamed their *hybris,* and defeat and humiliation have made them human. The new cosmic myth has touched them and brought them closer to all in the retribalization of the era. Informational decentralization has brought them out of their panel-lined board rooms, and the death of industrial capitalism has taken away the magic of the culture of wealth. With the elect living in cosmic indifference to the dinosaur-machines of the old technology, wealth has become *prima facie* evidence of mediocrity. Like the Headman, a Manager is a simple person trying to administer a very necessary but very colorless business. The Managers are slightly stunned by the sudden reversal of the old order, for they thought it was going to be the triumph of the routine-operational mentality forever. But they have been humbled only for a while; their day will return in a few centuries when the ideational charismatics will have played out their era. But at the beginning of Phase IV it is all the triumph of the Pythagorean, the Scientist-Shaman of the Aquarian Age, as Gavin Arthur of the San Francisco *Oracle* would phrase it.

In the first quadrant of the sphere of the Scientists is the coordinator, the man like Oppenheimer who can speak to other scientists and administer programs in ways no bureaucrat ever could. His complementary opposite across the sphere is the solitary visionary, a man like Einstein. Next to him on the charismatic side in the third quadrant is the theoretician, a Heisenberg or a Feynman. His complementary opposite across the sphere in the second quadrant is the technologist, the anonymous artisan among the multitudes of a Cape Kennedy.

This Scientific-Planetary Civilization may appear to be a source of light, but it is a light at the end of a long and very dark tunnel. There is always the chance that Phase IV may be, simply, the end. If this end is, however, merely the end to the civilization of the industrial nation-state (and that will be apocalyptic enough for those of us who expect to be around by the year 2000), then perhaps we can imagine a miscegenetic, planetary, and post-technological civilization arising on the ashes of the old order. Whatever the content of that future order, I expect its structure to be an expression of the eternal four. Even then opposites will continue to play out their roles in conflict, but out of that conflict, I still believe, a unity will emerge.

When one discovers a field effect to values and conflict, the immediate consequence is to be changed from an actor to an observer. All positions on the wheel seem unsatisfying and incomplete. It would seem that to realize values collectively in the tragedy of conflict, one has to be willing to throw his individuality away, for with every choice a person makes, he purchases his virtue with an inseparable vice. And even in withdrawing from the theater of conflict one is still involved in the tragic scheme, for he purchases knowledge at a price of inaction. To become conscious of the field, one must move into a different space off that wheel, but once off the wheel, one seems to be escaping the very condition of being human. Since the condition of being human is to be ignorant, violent, loving and hating, and charging blindly into cages and then screaming for freedom, the escape from being human is, as the

Lord Gautama pointed out a long time ago, not necessarily an evil thing. And yet as Yeats has said in "A Dialogue of Self and Soul," "And what's the good of an escape/If honour find him in the wintry blast?" Even the Buddhism of contemplation allowed for the Bodhisattvas of action. The artist, the man who lives at the interface between pure imagination and its material realization, perhaps best understands the paradoxical nature of action. "Act and remain apart from action," Yeats wrote to a friend in paraphrase of the Bhagavad-Gita after a lifetime of some fine fighting and some fine escaping. But even in escaping the artist is never alone, for whether it is Blake in obscurity, Yeats in his Tower, or Faulkner in Oxford, Mississippi, the eyes of civilization are turned toward him in his imagination. In solitude the artist escapes to nothing less than the space in which to create. But for all the privileges of the artist, he, too, like the rest of us, is strapped to the wheel and can say with King Lear:

> You do me wrong to take me out o' th' grave.
> Thou art a soul in bliss; but I am bound
> Upon a wheel of fire, that mine own tears
> Do scald like molten lead.

5

A.D. 2000: THE MILLENNIUM
UNDER NEW MANAGEMENT

"Major fighting in Viet Nam will peter out about 1967; and most objective observers will regard it as a substantial American victory. . . . In the United States Lyndon Johnson will have been reelected in 1968." Thus Professor Ithiel de Sola Pool, Chairman of Political Science at M.I.T., sees the beginning of the future in his "The International System in the Next Half Century."[1] His human lack of foresight only becomes disturbing when we are forced to consider his accuracy when he goes on to predict that "There will be no nuclear war within the next fifty years."

If Professor de Sola Pool had to stand alone, he might find his position extremely embarrassing, but it is the standard operating procedure of technocrats that they never work alone, but always gather in the committees of experts in which they are not individually held responsible. Just such a gathering of experts was called in 1965 and 1966 in the formation of the American Academy of Arts and Sciences' Commission on the Year 2000. A few were as young as thirty-five, but for the most part it was a gathering of like-minded, middle-aged, academic liberals. To compensate for their lack of diversity, their distinguished chairman, Daniel Bell, asked them to "think wild" in their imaginings of the year 2000. What they came up with was a fairly accurate picture of the year 1965, but what they came up with is not as important as why they came together in the first place.

It would seem that liberalism is entering a new age of expansion. Before, it had been content to negate the historicist visions of the past in a "piecemeal technology" that concerned itself with the here and now. But having defeated the old feudal-religious world view completely, it seems about to take on some of the characteristics of the former ruler— much in the way newly freed colonial nations take on the habits of their departed lords. Chiliasm, millenarian visions of the Second Coming, the end of history and the consummation of man, these were things that belonged to religion and the religious ages. Now liberalism is addressing itself to the future of man and announcing that it feels itself large enough to fill the void it has created. As one member of the Commission, Donald Schon, remarked: "Our process is more interesting than our product. The more interesting questions concern the ways in which our society can use the results of such deliberations. If predictions are going to be wrong, how can they be *organized* [my italics] so that they are wrong effectively?"[2]—which is about as good an example of liberal thinking as one could hope for.

Right and wrong, truth and falsehood are seen as naïve polarizations that distract one from the more important matter of academic organization. It is not the values that are imporant, but the social institutions they call into existence. It is a positive social value that so many distinguished American scholars are brought together through a generous grant from the Carnegie Corporation (another group of middle-aged, like-minded liberals) so that their informed deliberations can be made available through publication. If the opinions are wrong, then one can read the work in the light of what the experts thought in the 1965–67 period. Unfortunately, by giving up the hope and the risk of achieving anything of true value, the bureaucrat protects himself and thus ensures his failure. One cannot fall if he has never flown, and one cannot fly unless he has hurled himself into the air.

But let us take them at their word. Having settled unfairly on their most glaring failure in Professor de Sola Pool's prediction, let us give up the game of proving the experts to be wrong about the future and follow Mr. Schon's suggestion to look beyond the futuristic camouflage to see what is really going on in their immediate activities. One theme that runs through the papers and meetings of the Commission is the growing obsolescence of democracy in an age of technology. As Zbigniew Brzezinski remarks: "The government is conservative in relation to change because it generates essentially post-crisis management institutions. In order to create pre-crisis management institutions, in a setting which we would call political-democratic, we will have to increasingly separate the political system from society and begin to conceive of the two as separate entities."[3] To separate the way in which men relate to one another and to reify that way itself as something over and above the men themselves is to achieve the triumph of what Jacques Ellul calls "technique" by substituting the efficiency of systems for the experience of men.[4]

In order to separate people from the political system, one will have to lead them away for something else, and that is why it is so necessary to have a Commission on the Year 2000. The millennium is the technological promised land; it is an age in which technology has solved all the problems technology created, a time when clumsy postcrisis politics has been replaced by precrisis behavioral engineering. It is a time in which men have finally listened to sound advice and have turned over their political power to the experts to be cared for in a way that is truly best for them.

One member of the Commission, Erik Erikson, expressed a nervousness in taking part in its grand designs—no doubt because he sensed that what it was all about was power. An image of a great technological future was to be used to maintain control over society.

The traditional sources of identity strength—economic, racial, national, religious, occupational—are all in the process of allying themselves with a new world-image in which the vision of an anticipated future and, in fact, of a future in a permanent state of planning, will take over much of tradition.[5]

Just as once before the Churchmen offered a vision of salvation after a life of suffering, so now the priesthood of technocracy will offer a planned future 2000 for those caught in the agonies of the seventies. But there are new devils and irrational temptresses

standing between the present and the future, and so
the technocrats must be on their guard. As Daniel
Bell warned the Commission: "The tensions between the 'technocratic' and the 'apocalyptic' modes,
particularly among the intellectuals, may be one of
the great ruptures in moral temper, especially in the
universities." In order to maintain their power, the
experts must make it appear that all revolts against
technocracy are mindless, "mythic," and irrational
outbursts, and thus *prima facie* evidence of the need
for expert controls. Again, it was Erikson who ad-
dressed himself to Bell's political distinction:

Has not every major era in history been characterized
by a division into a new class of *power-specialists* (who
"know what they are doing") and an intense new group
of universalists (who "mean what they are saying")?
. . . It also seems reasonable to assume that without the
apocalyptic warnings of the universalist, the new technocrats might not have been shocked into restraining
the power they wield.[6]

The difficulty with the liberal imagination is that
it is so owned by the myth of progress that it cannot
think of the future in any other terms except more
of the same. In Stephen R. Graubard's article on
"University Cities in the Year 2000," he sees what
is basically a Cambridge, Massachusetts, with an
urban renewal program having cleared out the stores
and frame houses of the poor. M.I.T. and Harvard,
by A.D. 2000, have simply joined to squash Central
Square between them:

In university cities, faculty will not exist as a corporate group set apart. Their relations with other professional groups will be more regular. At a time when
London will be an hour's distance from New York,

scholars and teachers will divide their time between several university cities, teaching and studying regularly both in this country and abroad. This perpetual coming and going will render even more difficult than is now the case the creation of environments suited to contemplation and reflection. The bustle of university cities will not be welcome to all scholars; many will seek to pursue their work in greater isolation—even in rural retreats. The greatest number will, nevertheless, accept the inconveniences and find attractive the city's intellectual and social qualities. The university cities will emerge as principal centers of artistic and creative endeavour. They will support such talents, not least because they will provide an ample market for their product.[7]

The trouble with this idealized vision of Cambridge, 1966, is that it overlooks one simple *liberal* economic fact that could change a great deal. A guaranteed annual income, as Paul Goodman has pointed out, means that an individual can choose to opt out of the marketplace to live on a permanent fellowship, and most of the speculators on the Commission assume some sort of guaranteed annual income by the year 2000. This economic fact means that Harvard professors will not have to retreat to rural liberal arts colleges to find a pastoral vision of contemplation; they can stay on in Harvard Square and have students exactly as Socrates had them in the Agora of Athens. The university will most likely not grow into the size of a city, but will shrink as it realizes that it is the city itself (and not the campus) that is the true university. Given the fact that a technological culture can support a high percentage of dropouts, it is likely that the cities of the future will be teeming with sophists who will compete for the affections of the young. And, as happened before, the student will get what he deserves, Socrates or Gorgias, for no Harvard or M.I.T. will want to certify his choice. But all of this is, of course, assuming a linear progression of things as they are now. In the doubled, Yeatsian vision of history, a new charismatic institution is being born which will scorn the Pharaonic magnificence of Cambridge, 1966 or A.D. 2000.

Clearly, if the university-city is a supermarket and an informational service station, then wisdom, perhaps even knowledge, is not going to be found in it. The extreme routinization of the university will not result in more of the same, but in a charismatic reversal to the centers of the Dark Ages that preceded Oxford and Bologna. So linear is the Commission's sense of history that the proceedings read like the pronouncements of Europe's greatness and progress before 1914. Only two men seem to be profoundly uneasy in the presence of this positivism, Erik Erikson and David Reisman. It remained for Reisman to give voice to the anxiety that was becoming more evident to the sensitive as the Commission's work drew to a close:

It is characteristic of such discussions as ours in this country to forget that we fought a Civil War. It very seldom even lingers in our consciousness of the future. Perhaps it is as far behind us as the revolution that deposed Charles I in the seventeenth century is behind the British. Yet I keep doubting it; I keep feeling that our society consists of a series of interlocked deterrents and that by no means all lie in the government in power. . . . How is it that the National Guard from Mississippi will kill Mississippians if necessary? Why is it that the

telephone company is not able to control its Mississippi
operators who give out the unlisted telephone numbers
of "nigger-lovers" who are being besieged by obscene
phone calls, who change their numbers, and who the
next day find that the number is again in the hands of
the besiegers? It seems to me that McNamara's military
control, to which reference was made earlier, is by no
means firm. The suspicion often crosses my mind that
every time he closes down a base he has to give General
Westmoreland another division, or the Navy another
carrier. We grealty underplay the degree to which we
are still a decentralized, chaotic, anarchic society in
which the government has extraordinary powers in some
spheres, a kind of plebiscitary or Populist power. There
are, on the other hand, sabotaging, deterring powers in
a very complicated relationship. The future is more
opaque, more chaotic perhaps than our general thinking
suggests when we see only the mechanisms of control,
intimidation, and power, and not the mechanisms of
sabotage and deterrence.[8]

Alan Pifer, the president of the Carnegie Corporation (and the man who was, therefore, financing the
Commission), responded to Reisman's warning in
the following manner: "I was particularly interested
in the discussion that aparently took place in the
group that Leonard Duhl reported on and which
dealt with the process of national planning. This is
an issue that needs a great deal more thought and
exploration." And so the scab closed over the wound
Riesman had opened; a few seconds later, even the
scab was gone and the smooth and plastic flesh
smiled on and nodded in mutual congratulation for
the stimulation all had received in the preceedings.
Vowing to have more wild thinking sessions in the
near future, they adjourned.

II

What is lacking in the proceedings of the American Academy of Arts and Sciences' Commission on the Year 2000 is a vision of terror and an understanding of evil. On the ideational side of the liberal sphere, the liberal humanists like Riesman and Erikson tried to deepen the understanding of the operational liberals, but to no avail. Because the liberal humanist believes in institutional rationalization and in working from within, he is only too easily rendered impotent by the masters of procedures and routines. Liberal humanists are men of good will, but like the benevolent Owenite capitalists who sought to check the power of industrialists, they are beautiful orchids growing in a jungle. The appeal "to work within the system" is always sounded by the systems managers for they know well that the mass of the liberal humanists is nothing against the inertial mass of the system itself. Once again the historical irony appears that all things end up in the position opposite to their beginning. The beginning of liberalism with Locke was a movement away from throne and altar into the new free spaces of the market and the school. Now at the point of its complete development, we are bound to corporation and machine. The *genius loci* of this era in which the school and the market are one is, of course, the new operational liberal, the technocrat. And one of the most eminent members of this new breed of liberal is Herman Kahn.

If the Commission fell short of reality because it lacked an understanding of terror, one would expect that Herman Kahn could well make up the difference. The author of *On Thinking the Unthinkable* and the man who put the word "megadeaths" into the English language is certainly the man who can look into the eye of thermonuclear war and, without blinking, take the shroud measurements of the corpse of civilization. But, surprisingly enough, Kahn, too, succumbs to the general positivism of the sixties and only toys with apocalypse. For him, too, the future is more of the same, and in his Hudson Institute's study, *The Year 2000: A Framework for Speculation on the Next Thirty-Three Years,* he sees the future in a linear extrapolation of the following "multifold trend":

There is a basic, long-term multifold trend toward:

1. Increasingly Sensate (empirical, this worldly, secular, humanistic, pragmatic, utilitarian, contractual, epicurean or hedonistic, and the like) cultures
2. Bourgeois, bureaucratic, "meritocratic," democratic (and nationalistic?) elites
3. Accumulation of scientific and technological knowledge
4. Institutionalization of change, especially research, development, innovation, and diffusion
5. Worldwide industrialization and modernization
6. Increasing affluence and (recently) leisure
7. Population growth
8. Urbanization and (soon) the growth of megalopolises
9. Decreasing importance of primary and (recently) secondary occupations
10. Literacy and education
11. Increasing capability for mass destruction
12. Increasing tempo of change
13. Increasing universality of the multifold trend.[9]

Mr. Kahn takes into account the probable appearance of nativistic revolts against technology, but he does not see these as becoming sufficiently effective to alter the basic, multifold trend. He and Anthony Weiner see the twentieth-century Luddites as being as ineffective as their nineteenth-century predecessors; the Technological Revolution in America will roll over protest just as the Industrial Revolution did in Great Britain. The liberal industrial world view will spread until all the undeveloped nations are under its polluted sky.

In any case it seems plausible that the "end of ideology" and an inevitable disenchantment with the ideals and expectations of American democracy and free enterprise, coupled with a continued decline in the influence of traditional religion and the absence of any acceptable mass ideologies, have and will continue to contribute to a common spiritual and political rootlessness. As secularization, rationalization, and innovation continue to change the culture in the direction of Sensate and bourgeois norms, the influence of traditional Weltanschauungen seems more likely to continue to wane than undergo any resurgence in the next thirty-three years.[10]

Kahn's and Weiner's view of the future is a very predictable one, for it is only human for a writer to expect that history will grow in his direction. The liberal feels that liberal values will become increasingly triumphant; the powerless fundamentalist feels that apocalypse will tumble the proud and mighty into the dust, and that he will be found living in the truth. Few on either the Left or the Right ever imagine that they will both be right, and that in the supra-ideological process of history events will be as profoundly ambiguous as existence has always been. The Industrial Revolution, in the words of the title of a recent textbook, is at once a triumph and a disaster. The liberals point to what they want to see in terms of progress; the conservatives and the radicals point to the price it cost in the individual, society, and the environment. The Technological Revolution, no doubt, will prove itself to be the worthy son of its father, and the curses and the blessings will be passed on. So it is not so strange at all that an established technocrat like Herman Kahn should see history as moving in the terms of his liberal, multifold trend. We are all magnets and what is locked in our fields of consciousness is merely the "facts" we attract. Another mind, say one like Heisenberg's, might look at modern history and see that far more important than the obvious mass multifold trend is an elite movement away from materialism into an increasingly Platonic view in which the structure of energy and consciousness is revealed in profoundly anti-materialistic *forms*. What is secondary for one is primary to the other; what is evidence of spectacular accent to the technocrat is evidence of the prelude to an equally spectacular fall for the apocalyptist.

But what is surprising about Kahn's world view is its utter dearth of imagination. When Kahn looks at the millennium, all he can see, in positive terms, is the growth of the Gross National Products of the major powers; and, in negative terms, thermonuclear war, human evolutionary stagnation, and irrational nativistic revolts. The GNP's of the major powers may increase, or the International Monetary Fund may collapse; since optimism is more congenial to the positivism of the liberal ideology, it is more efficient to be optimistic. It is also more efficient because the technocrats are the rulers, and to hold onto their power they must offer us a renewed faith in the system through the prospect of increasing prosperity.

One wishes, however, that while the liberals were imagining astounding growth in the GNP, they might envision other achievements of civilization. Seventeen hundred and seventy saw the beginning of the Industrial Revolution, but it also saw the beginning of the movement of Romanticism, which, as a movement in European culture, had a fairly profound effect on human history, artistic and political. Will the future see some equivalent rise of man's imaginative powers to challenge and outrace his technological actions, or will the increasingly "Sensate" multifold trend result in a new human culture in which the purpose of human existence is seen in the uplifting of the Gross World Product? Since Kahn and Weiner look at the nonmaterialistic spheres of human culture as mere ideology, it is not surprising that they overlook everything but the future of the managers and the threats to the managers contained in ideological movements.

But for all their lack of imagination, one great quality that Kahn's and Weiner's extensive study has over the proceedings of the Commission (to which they contributed a small portion of their work) is that it is willing to take terror into account in its view of the future. Here, no doubt, Kahn's experience with the RAND Corporation and the military has given him a larger perspective than that of the ordinary academic.

To start with small terrors and work up to larger ones, there is the prospect that as the Technological Society expands it is likely to generate irrational reactions. In the liberal tradition of the historical scholarship of Norman Cohn,[11] Kahn and Weiner see these reactionary movements as "totalitarian":

> Among primitive societies placed in situations of great stress, the phenomenon of redemptive mass movements has been most nakedly magical and naïve. The totalitarian movements of modern Europe have (or had) highly sophisticated rationales, although their ultimate objectives defied reason. But it could be argued that there is a common impulse in all of these, that the kind of social crisis that produced them will deepen in Asia during the next thirty years, not be reduced, and to expect that we have seen the end of such movements even in the advanced societies of the West must constitute an act of faith in human reason and progress rather than an argument from evidence.[12]

Nazism is, of course, a prime example of a totalitarian movement, but A. F. C. Wallace, who wrote the classic article on these stress-engendered "revitalization movements,"[13] is more open-minded and recognizes that many positive movements in political liberation and religious revitalization have originated in the structural process Kahn and Weiner reduce to "totalitarian." Revitalization movements constitute a threat to empire, and, therefore, they must be dealt with severely. Kahn's and Weiner's scholarship here is clearly politically movitated, for one can make a much stronger case that it is the Technological Society that is totalitarian, for it reduces all cultures to mere ideological impediments to the advance of "rationalization." Technology is "total" because it sees everything other than itself as reactionary, irrational, and primitive. The inversion of values by which Kahn and Weiner seek to nullify the force of the attack against them by branding libertarian movements as totalitarian shows clearly how their "rational" science is merely a weapon in the hands of a ruling elite. The tragedy of this situation comes from the fact that a New Left popular attack against them will gain such momentum that rational science will indeed become a target, and attacks on Kahn and Weiner and their Hudson Institute will not be scrupulously aimed at merely the guilty.

The scientific pretensions of Kahn and Weiner in particular and technocrats in general have brought about a tragic fall of science into industrial technology. In the double-bind condition of original sin, we have moved away from Swift's Academy of Legado to M.I.T. and the Hudson Institute. Their charts and grafts may give the appearance of being more scientific than my merely literary essays, but if one takes a simple-minded, linear extrapolation and puts it through several computer runs, he is still going to come out with a simple-minded, linear extrapolation of the GNP's of the major powers in A.D. 2000. All the computers in the world won't help you if your unexamined and unconscious assumptions on the nature of reality are simply wrong in their basic conception. All the computers can do is help you to be stupid in an expensive fashion. Kahn and Weiner are no more scientific than the actors on late-night television, who with trappings of white laboratory smocks, charts, graphs, and acidity meters try to "prove" that Rolaids can cure the upset stomach the commercial is causing.

Precisely because Kahn and Weiner are neither scientists nor humanists, but what we call social scientists, they have difficulty in understanding human forms of violence and terror in their revolutionary aspects and can only find themselves at home in discussions of the technological forms of violence and terror inflicted upon men by their own machines. Here Kahn and Weiner come into their own and become quite effectively frightening as they discuss the military-political world which they serve. Kahn does not feel that there will be thermonuclear war in the next thirty years, but to be on the safe side, he offers some possible scenarios for its occurrence. But thermonuclear war is only the grossest form of technological threat, and Kahn has been close enough to the military to know that there are more subtle forms of mechanized violence.

Greater wealth and improved technology give us a wider range of alternatives; but once an alternative has been chosen, much regulation and imposed order is needed. Thus with geometric increase in the complexity and organization of modern life, corresponding, even if not directly proportional, increases in the scope and complexity of human and organizational controls will become necessary. One need not assume the triumph of the police mentality, or the intrusion of motivation denigrative of human dignity, to foresee this. Each restriction will have its valid and attractive rationale, which may even be libertarian. Federal safety regulations for automobile manufacturers and tests for drivers today increase the "freedom" of the license-holding driver to drive in safety. Coercive treatment for the mentally ill raises the probability that they will be able to lead freely constructive lives. Plastic hearts may replace real ones and *damaged brains may be linked to computers.* [My italics; see comment in Notes.] Therapeutic abortions, through the death of the foetus, increase the freedom of the mother. And the biological adaptation of man to his ecological niche in an extremely complicated and overpopulated society will increase his freedom to live a satisfying and useful life.

We have, of course, omitted the crucial qualification, under the existent conditions. It is still possible that the terminus of the process may be inconsistent with anything we would regard as freedom or dignity, or even human. The evolution of society may produce the devolution of man. The adaptability (and superiority) of man has heretofore consisted in his lack of specialized adaptation (as in the case of lesser animals). Man may, in the not-so-distant future, be adapted in a specialized sense, while society through the control of genetic science maintains its general adaptability by fitting men to the varying tasks that time and environment provide. (Thus the survival of the fittest may be replaced by the fitting of the survivors.)[14]

Perhaps because it is so hard to think about thermonuclear war, I find such visions of our immediate future far more terrifying. Statements like "To the extent to which humankind is permitted to persist it may be kept in a perpetually drugged and/or subservient state" are more frightening because they seem to be only a slight exaggeration of the present drugged condition of middle-class and hippie America. We are already in a trap in which we are using more technology to save us from our technologically created predicaments. We are not even beginning to move into that intellectual clarity which Ivan Illich describes as the moment of understanding when we abandon our "solutions" as we let go of the illusions that made them necessary.[15] Rather than re-visioning our predicament into what T. S. Eliot called "a condition of complete simplicity costing no less than everything," we are rushing, like lemmings to the sea, into alcohol, pot, headache pills, tranquilizers, speed, and LSD. We follow an insane life and diet that cause heart disease, and then seek to cure the symptoms through heart transplants. Regarding the body as a machine of interchangeable parts, we ignore the signs that scream at us that it is an organism, and then forcibly suppress rejection with powerful drugs. The drugs, in turn, upset the organism's defenses against similar attacks, so then we have to introduce more artificial defenses that only further obviate the body's system. As long as we fail to step back and call into question our most basic assumptions, there is no other way to go but deeper and deeper into the trap: a body of artificial parts will only be a temporary and imperfect version of the Cyborg, but the technicians will labor on until they achieve the perfect "Machine That Is Man."[16]

Of course, there will be a few who will be disturbed by the suicidal culture of technology, but if people can be made to think that there is something cool and pastoral about smoking Salem cigarettes in front of the radiation from a color TV set, then there is no reason to think that the protestors will be looked upon as anything other than "disturbed." And these will be the mentally disturbed people who will create the nativistic revolts that Kahn and Weiner predict will be as ineffectual as the Luddite attacks upon the stocking frames. The victims of Technological Society, the great silent majority, will pour out their anxiety and fear in a rage which politicians will be able to direct away from themselves and onto the irrational troublemakers. Brzezinski's precrisis management will save the ex-citizens from the crises the system produced, and will continue to produce in order to refine its own techniques of crisis-creation and crisis-resolution. But the conservative liberals will not be able to last forever with the Greek colonels' style of Agnew, Mitchell, and Nixon. Eventually the progressive liberals will return to reinstitute the New Government of Youth. In their mod clothes and sensitivity-trained style, the new managers will understand the needs of a complex, postindustrial culture: the last vestige of puritanical America will be swept away and in the new Empire they shall have psychedelic TV and legal pot.

History is the lie commonly agreed upon.
VOLTAIRE

6

THE RE-VISIONING
OF HISTORY

Since the Commission on the Year 2000 failed to
take Daniel Bell's advice to "think wild," I intend
to do so now. The difficulty with Daniel Bell and
Herman Kahn, and their view of the future, is that
they lack the imagination to see the whole wheel of
fire and can only view reality from the very limited
perspective of the routine-operational mentality.
They are simply blind to anything that is not supportive of the liberal-industrial world view. In the
terms of Karl Mannheim's "sociology of knowledge"
they express only an "ideology":

> The concept "ideology" reflects the one discovery
> which emerged from political conflict, namely, that rul-
> ing groups can in their thinking become so intensively
> interest-bound to a situation that they are simply no
> longer able to see certain facts which would undermine
> their sense of domination. There is implicit in the word
> "ideology" the insight that in certain situations the col-
> lective unconscious of certain groups obscures the real
> condition of society both to itself and to others and
> thereby stabilizes it.[1]

If the Commissioners had tried to reach out beyond the perspectives of the professional classes, they

might have discovered that in 1967 the most widely read view of the year 2000 was that of Edgar Cayce as popularized in Jess Stearn's best-seller, *The Sleeping Prophet*.[2] Our democratic society is so stratified that one level can be totally ignorant of what is going on in the other. The professional upper-middle class is caught up with Daniel Bell and Herman Kahn, but the lower-middle (or just plain middle) class is filling up with the occult prophecies of Cayce, which now, thanks to Stearn's year-long best-seller, are available to them in over a dozen paperback books. Bookstores frequented by far-out students and hippies have special sections filled with Cayce's books, as well as other old occult classics that have taken on a new life in Aquarian Age culture. When viewed with all the occult books and objects,[3] the Cayce phenomenon amounts to a cultural syndrome, and yet I have encountered only one academic who was aware of Cayce. If, as Mannheim suggests, classes can be so interest-bound that they cannot perceive reality outside of the terms that sustain their power, then it is extremely important that we adopt an alien point of view—if only to open our minds and free us of the ethnocentrism of our former position.

The prophecies of fundamentalist Edgar Cayce are about as alien a perspective as one could hope for in relation to the perspective of Cambridge, U.S.A. Cayce's vision is the timeless pastoral one of the rural, powerless prophet against the powerful but dying cities. Amos wrote his sermons, but Cayce, the uneducated country boy from Hopkinsville, Kentucky, went into a trance and there answered the questions put to him about cures for the sick, world events, religion, science, and the future. According to Stearn, Cayce predicted both world wars, the Depression, and then-unknown phenomena like the periodic reversal of the earth's magnetic field—parenthetically while trying to find a cure for a patient. But what has brought Cayce back into attention since his death in 1945 is his predictions for the last third of the twentieth century. In the best pastoral tradition of prophecy, the most urban and technologically advanced parts of the world are lined up for destruction by cataclysmic earthquakes and rising coastal waters: California, New York City, Japan, and Scandinavia. Just as man was proclaiming he now dominated nature, nature was about to wake up from her twelve-thousand-year-old slumber and shake the flies off her back. All the horrors of the technologically controlled society that Kahn envisioned for the twenty-first century would have to be postponed as man once again turned from the destruction of himself to waging a desperate war against his most ancient adversary.

If one were going to write history as tragic drama, Cayce's material would furnish many great ironies. Man had fought a severe battle with nature in the Stone Age, and then nature quit the field; but just as man was about to use his technology to change his human nature, nature returned and man became involved in a battle with all the contradictions of that oxymoron, "human nature." And just as man was about to destroy himself in thermonuclear war and the industrial destruction of the ecological system of the planet, natural cataclysms came and distracted him from war and eliminated the pollution in Califor-

nia, Scandinavia, and Japan. Reading Cayce with
an eye for artistic structures, one cannot help but
wonder what effect a Cayce scenario for the year
2000 would have on North American civilization. As
Freud observed: "One of the few gratifying and exalt-
ing impressions which mankind can offer is when, in
the face of elemental catastrophe, it forgets the dis-
cordancies of its civilization and all its internal
difficulties and animosities, and recalls the great common task of preservng itself against the superior
power of nature."⁴

Great and terrible as Cayce's prediction of the
destruction of millions upon millions of people is,
it is only part of the upheaval of the new age. As the
ground opened up before his feet, man, in discovering
that the geological doctrine of uniformitarianism was
false, was also going to wonder if cataclysms had
ever occurred before. Legends of destroyed civilizations would take on a new look of possibility. Appropriately enough, Cayce speaks about Atlantis and
Lemuria, for in diagnosing patients he had found the
roots of their disease in previous incarnations in
these lost civilizations. Upon waking, and reading the
record of his trance, Cayce found the lost Atlantis
buried in his own unconscious. Going back into
trance later, he began to explore the question and
prophesied that in the last third of the twentieth
century the remains of Atlantis would be discovered
in the Bahamas and that history would prove larger
than any of the university historians had imagined.

Once before, according to Cayce, a high civilization had reached great scientific heights and then
destroyed the very basis of its civilization through

its own technology. The crystals that were used to focus cosmic rays were tuned too high, and the magnetic field of the inner mantle and the crust of the earth itself were affected; Atlantis sank and what was left survived in the New World civilizations and in the Near East with the bits and pieces of the old technology and the old Pythagorean science. In Cayce's tragic vision, the Hindu law of karma is still in force and the souls of the Atlanteans have re-incarnated in America in a time that is so structurally similar to their previous condition that they can work out their salvation once again. From Cayce's visionary perspective, because we are ignorant of the history of Atlantis, we are doomed to repeat it. Here the vision of Cayce seems remarkably similar to the visions of Blake, a man the unlettered Cayce presumably did not read. As Professor Northrop Frye interprets Blake:

> The fall of Albion included a deluge in which the center of Atlantis was overwhelmed and only the fragments of the British Isles were left. The settlement of America by the English and revolt of America against the dead hand of English tyranny is therefore the dawn of a new age in which Atlantis begins to appear above the waves.[5]

Once again technology is affecting the very basis of a civilization, and once again a spiritual crisis is splitting the society into two opposing sides: for Blake, the sides of Orc and Urizen. Before, Cayce claims, the Atlanteans had genetically altered the apes so that they could serve as android-slaves (a project that is once again being talked about by genetic engineers); then a religious group arose and claimed that since their evolutionary rate of ascent had been altered, they were now human and should be freed and considered as souls. The powerful Atlanteans rejected their claims, entrenched their own position with further evils, and pushed on headlong toward disaster. Groups of the protestors fled to Mexico and South America and waited for the end they could see coming.

Reading Cayce, if not as good as reading William Blake, is as good as most science fiction,[6] and it is easy to see why the hippies I met in Big Sur wove him into a metahistory that included Tolkien's *Lord of the Rings*. Cayce's Atlantis is Tolkien's Númenor, complete with the same astral magic, extraterrestrial Valar, strange crystals, and the great crisis that sends the good refugees all over the world. It is all an entertaining fantasy that thrills the reader all the more because it pretends to be more than fiction. But as the fantasy crops up in several clearly separated traditions, it begins to insinuate its way into the reader's imagination until it becomes slightly unsettling. At the back of one's head a thought begins to push toward the front of one's consciousness: *What if the history of the world is "a myth," but myth is the remains of the real history of earth?* The neat inversion of "reality" is so fictionally effective that one shivers at the thought of the social cost of taking it seriously. Suddenly the dilemma of Oedipa Maas, the heroine of Pynchon's *Crying of Lot 49,* takes on a new reality: gestalt pattern forms a whole "antiworld"; the pieces of reality stay in their places, but the whole articulating configuration shifts into another dazzlingly complete world view:

With her own eyes she [Oedipa] had verified a WASTE system: seen two WASTE postmen, a WASTE mailbox, WASTE stamps, WASTE cancellations. And the image of the muted post horn all but saturating the Bay Area. Yet she wanted it all to be fantasy—some clear result of her several wounds, needs, dark troubles. She wanted Hilarius to tell her she was some kind of nut and needed a rest, and that there was no Trystero. She also wanted to know why the chance of its being real should menace her so.[7]

Quickly one blinks his eyes to set the pattern back into its "real" form, hurls the thought to the back of his mind, and then rushes on to other things. But if fate has ordered it that story time for the children should, accidentally, turn out to be C. S. Lewis' *Chronicles of Narnia*—or, for light summer reading for oneself, his science fiction trilogy—then all the blinking is for nothing. The patterned antiworld remains. Like Oedipa, one can only feel as if he is the victim of a conspiracy. What secret conspiracy against modernism has caused Tolkien and Lewis to interlock their works around the fantasies of the mythic past and the science fiction fantasies of the equally mythic present and future? Or is the conspiracy merely Christianity? Is that what that religion and these religious authors are all about? For C. S. Lewis, at least, Christianity is more than myth and symbol. His prophecy is direct and *ultimately* political:

God will invade. But I wonder whether people who ask God to interfere openly and directly in our world quite realize what it will be like when he does. When that happens, it is the end of the world. When the author walks on to the stage the play is over. God is going to invade, all right: but what is the good of saying you are on His side then, when you see the whole natural universe melting away like a dream and something else—something it never entered your head to conceive—comes crashing in; something so beautiful to some of us and so terrible to others that none of us will have any choice left?[8]

Lewis' understanding of the subversive power of children's literature is clearly expressed (for the adult reading it to the child) in the second volume of the Narnia series, *Prince Caspian*. This young prince, who is to inherit the throne from his evil uncle, is intentionally raised in an environment in which no fairy tales or legends are permitted. But one nurse violates the rule and tells the young prince all the great legends of Narnia—legends that we, from the first volume, know to be the actual history of the kingdom. Caspian's usurping people do not want the true story to be known, for it is subversive of their power. The evil uncle is disturbed at the way Caspian is growing up and at last decides to go ahead with his secret desires to take the kingdom away from his nephew and give it to his own son. Caspian is warned by his tutor, who is a magician in disguise, and he flees for his life. Once out of the kingdom of his wicked uncle, he is out of its "reality" as well and he discovers that the old legends are really true. If, in the early volumes, Lewis is allegorizing our present historical condition, he unwraps the allegory in the later volumes. In the sixth volume, *The Magician's Nephew,* Atlantis appears in its own right. "The box was Atlantean; it came from the lost island of Atlantis. That meant it was centuries older than any of the stone-age things they dig up in Europe. And it wasn't a rough, crude thing like them either. For in the very dawn of time Atlantis was already a great city with palaces and temples and learned men."[9]

Lewis' and Tolkien's Oxford attack on the modern machine age is not novel, but it is subtle and clever. By saying, in effect, "Of course, all this is rubbish and nonsense, but it is entertaining," they can sneak unnoticed into the iron palace of technology. By speaking in a trance, Cayce was always out of hearing for all except "the lunatic fringe." And by declaiming in prophets' robes forty-eight years ago, D. H. Lawrence ensured that his vision of history would be overlooked in favor of his more popular Lady Jane and John Thomas:

I honestly think that the great pagan world of which Egypt and Greece were the last living terms, the great pagan world which preceded our era, once had a vast and perhaps perfect science of its own, a science in terms of life. In our era this science crumbled into magic and charlatanry. But even wisdom crumbles.

I believe that this great science previous to ours and quite different in constitution and nature from our science once was universal, established all over the then existing globe. I believe it was esoteric, invested in a large priesthood. Just as mathematics and mechanics and physics are defined and expounded in the same way in the universities of China or Bolivia or London or Moscow today, so, it seems to me, in the great world previous to ours a great science and cosmology were taught esoterically in all countries of the globe, Asia, Polynesia, Atlantis, and Europe. . . .

In that world men lived and taught and knew, and were in one complete correspondence over all the earth. Men wandered back and forth from Atlantis to the

Polynesian Continent as men now sail from Europe to America. The interchange was complete, and knowledge, science was universal over the earth, cosmopolitan as it is today.

Then came the melting of the glaciers, and the world flood. The refugees from the drowned continents fled to the high places of America, Europe, Asia, and the Pacific Isles. And some degenerated naturally into cave men, neolithic and paleolithic creatures, and some retained their marvelous innate beauty and life-perfection, as the South Sea Islanders, and some wandered savage in Africa, and some, like Druids or Etruscans or Chaldeans or Amerindians or Chinese, refused to forget, but taught the old wisdom, only in its half-forgotten forms. More or less forgotten, as knowledge: remembered as ritual, gesture, and myth-story.[10]

If Daniel Bell really wanted to "think wild," all he would have to do would be to invert reality and say, with the fairy tales and legends, that myth is history, our history a "myth." One can understand why Professor Bell might hesitate, for the price the university professor would have to pay for such an inversion would be rather high. If one is a teenage hippie, or a lower-class fundamentalist, or a famous, but notoriously crank artist, then it doesn't matter whether or not he believes in the lost continent of Atlantis, for he consitutes no threat to the university-accepted version of history. But if a historian or an archaeologist were to entertain such fantasies, he would find himself ostracized by his colleagues and scholarly associations, his tenure questioned, and his publishers threatened with massive university boycotts of their textbooks if they continued to publish his books. If somehow the scholar managed to find an "unreputable" publisher or journal to accept his work, he would discover that his writings had been myster- iously deleted from the annual bibliographies. Such, in fact, has been the fate of such proponents of the cataclysmic theory of prehistory as Dr. Immanuel Velikovsky and Dr. Manson Valentine. In scientific society the doctrine of geological uniformitarianism had won out only after a long and difficult battle with the theological pseudo science of the nineteenth cen- tury. It was, therefore, absolutely maddening to have twentieth-century catastrophists musing on the Flood as if the nineteenth century had never happened. Unfortunately, the catastrophists were not the only ones afflicted with short memories. The scientists also forgot that they, too, were once persecuted for violat- ing dogma and an imprimatur was once required for scientific publications. But the faults of orthodoxy are as present in science as religion: the scientists formed an Inquisition of right thinkers and threatened to interfere with Macmillan's university textbook mar- ket. The publishers gave in and Velikovsky's book was eliminated from their list.[11]

With the postwar growth of university populations and bureaucracies, it is not surprising that freedom of thought should be suppressed, for there are only so many original thinkers available, and they are never enough to man all the slots within a university department. Inevitably, the university must depend on "professional" competence instead of intellectual excellence to carry it through in the day-to-day busi- ness of training majors. But, once again, the double- bind condition means that in raising the bottom to the middle for professional competence, we must also depress the top. The tragedy of history repeats itself,

for the university that was once persecuted and controlled by the church has now become the church of
the technocratic world. The Galileos of today are not
likely to be kneeling before cardinals and mumbling
the truth under their breath; they will be kneeling
before professors with tenure. And so the university
will go about its *business,* while a new race of intellectuals grows up outside it to challenge its imaginative ability to create. Unfortunately for all of us, it
will be extremely difficult to distinguish the charlatan
from the original thinker. The tragic condition of
double-bind will be as true outside the university
as it is within.

But now we are being forced to make a decision
about charlatans and original thinkers, for one of
Cayce's prophecies seems to have come true. Cayce
predicted that parts of Atlantis would be discovered
as the land around the Bahamas slowly began to
rise. "Expect it in sixty-eight and sixty-nine. Not so
far away."[12] In 1967 Dimitri Rebikoff, while flying
in the Bahamas, sighted a submerged rectangular
structure a quarter of a mile in length. He discussed
his observation with Dr. Manson Valentine, but when
they returned to examine the site, the shifting sands
of the Grand Bahamian Bank had once again covered
the structure. Then in the spring of 1968 a Florida
cargo pilot named Robert Brush discovered what
looked like a sunken quadrangle or building off the
coast of Bimini—exactly where Cayce said such
formations would appear.[13] Once again Rebikoff and
Valentine went out to check on the sighting. From
his work in paleoentomology for a period of forty
years, Dr. Valentine was convinced of continental

drift and the cataclysmic theory of prehistory.[14] Since his professional colleagues were not exactly open to these notions, he was keenly interested in discovering solid artifactual evidence for his theories. What they found were sunken quadrangles and long stone lines which were either paved roads or the tops of huge, cyclopean walls. Now Dr. Valentine is engaged in preparing a book on his research, and Mr. Rebikoff, a specialist in underwater exploration, is continuing with the field work. The magnetism of Atlantis, however, has attracted many adventurers, each eager to beat out the other in finding Cayce's "fire crystal" of Atlantis. Because the orthodox archaeologists in the universities will not touch the subject in peril of excommunication, the site is open to all those who work outside "the discipline" of archeology. Ostracized scholars and amateurs are not the only ones at work in the area, for now there are explorers, scuba enthusiasts, one Count, and a few millionaires with enough money to allow them to play at being ostracized scholars, explorers, and adventurers.

It is hard to say what will come of it all, and although I have no intention of taking the burden of proof off Rebikoff's and Valentine's shoulders, I do think their work should be considered within the confines of the university.[15] (And here one should remember that in the last great controversy over prehistory and evolution it was the universities who were fighting the preposterous theories of Darwin and Huxley.) When one considers Valentine's papers with Charles Hapgood's recent study of the Piri Re'is map of 1513 that shows spherical trigonometric projections and accurate mapping of Antarctica *be-*

fore the present ice formation, he begins to suspect that we have literally reached the edge of history as we have known it in the universities. From his analysis of the enigmatic Piri Re'is map, Professor Hapgood is willing to begin the re-visioning of history:

The idea of the simple linear development of society from the culture of the paleolithic (Old Stone Age) through the successive stages of the neolithic (New Stone Age), Bronze, and Iron Ages must be given up. Today we find primitive cultures co-existing with advanced modern society on all the continenst. . . . We shall now assume that, some 20,000 years ago, while paleolithic peoples held out in Europe, more advanced cultures existed elsewhere on the earth, and that we have inherited a part of what they once possesseed, passed down from people to people.[16]

When one adds Hapgood's work on the Piri Re'is map to the work of Professors von Dechend and de Santillana at M.I.T. on the incredible sophistication of archaic astronomy and its technical language, myth,[17] he can see that there are many tatters in the whole cloth of history that a real Atlantis would help to explain. But as a cultural historian I am not yet in a position to prove anything. Yet even hunches have their place in responsible scientific research, for there have been times when the physicist knew there just had to be a missing, undiscovered particle if the pattern in front of his mind's eye was to make any sense at all. History is not making the sense it once seemed to make, and we seem to be in the position of the eighteenth century when fossils were being discovered but nobody knew what to make of them.

The first reaction was, naturally, to dismiss them, since they were subversive of orthodox history. They were therefore classed as *lusus naturae,* tricks of nature placed in the soil by the Devil to tempt the devout Christian away from the Biblical scheme.

In the nineteenth century no one suspected that underneath the Babylonians was the even more ancient culture of the Sumerians. Now that we believe that "History begins at Sumer," we may be startled once again to find that underneath the Sumerians are the far more ancient Atlanteans— which is exactly what the Sumerians tell us in their mythology. Bits and pieces of a new world view seem to lie scattered around us, and as suddenly the imagination perceives them in a new form, the old world view seems all the more incredible. Still, imagination is not knowledge; we do not *know* anything yet, but I would be willing to go out on a limb to say that I now believe that myth is the detritus of actual history, even if I do not yet know the new limits on my now widened horizon. Psychologically, I think the "repetition-compulsion" of all the variations of the Atlantis myth in children's stories, cartoons, comic books, fantasies, occult literature, and science fiction indicates that the catastrophe, though suppressed in history, remained in "memory traces" of the collective unconscious. Where once the Jungian, literary approach to myth and symbol satisfied me, I now think the archaeological remains make Jung seem too belletristic.

At the beginning of a study we do not need to *know* all the answers through *conclusive* proof; we do need to have an imaginatively open mind so that the *incipient* proof is not cast aside in a firm conviction that the experts will take care of everything. Darwin, Marx, and Freud challenged the experts and suffered for it; now that there are Darwinians, Marxists, and Freudians, *they* will have to be challenged as we look in new places for new ideas. As incipient evidence of our need to re-vision history, I would like to list the following problem areas in our contemporary view of man and his past.

I. THE PROBLEM OF EVOLUTION

I remember how startled I was in 1967 when Professor Robert Ockner (now at the University of California Hospital in San Francisco) told me he did not accept the theory of human evolution as proved because he thought it was an enormous overgeneralization on very fragmentary data. "The truth," he said with a smile, "is probably somewhere between the Bible and Darwin." I was very surprised because I always thought, without question, that only ignorant hicks from the South or Jehovah's Witnesses questioned the theory, and since I saw myself as definitely on the side of science against orthodox religion, I positioned myself in the matter without a thought for what was really only a matter of snobbery.

And, in fact, this kind of snobbery seems to have been one of the historical conditions which enabled the theory to triumph: the Victorian liberals were quick to champion the new theory because it helped them put the staid, port-sipping, fox-hunting, Tory clergy in its place. Loren Eiseley has recalled how vehemently Darwin reacted to Wallace's questioning of their joint theory. Even at the time of its formulation Wallace wondered why, if survival of the fittest was the mechanism of natural selection, man ever evolved a brain a hundred times more complex than that needed for survival. " 'No adequate explanation,' they confess over eighty years after Darwin scrawled his vigorous 'No' upon Wallace's paper, 'has been put forward to account for so large a cerebrum in man.' "[18] Five hundred thousand years ago, Pithecanthropus "evolved" with an explosion of brain size and frontal development. Since there are more primitive man-apes farther back, in the few remains of bones we have, it is tempting to connect the dots in a line that cuts across all the dimensions of plentiful space. It is all the more tempting to connect the dots in this way if one is living in an empire that places the white race at the end of a long line of progress in which the darker races are but bestial prefigurings of the Englishman. And if one lives in an economic system in which the market is red in tooth and claw, it is tempting to think that *laissez faire* and survival of the fittest are part of nature's way.

There are many reasons, in the sociology of knowledge, why a Victorian liberal would find Darwin's theory a welcome tool in his own bitter struggle for survival, just as there are many reasons why I would find the questioning of history a welcome tool in the struggle against the modern technocratic liberal. These ideas are connected to our nerves, and so we shall have to move very carefully, and the best one can argue for is a healthy skepticism that is still interested in finding answers. For the issue really is in doubt; as the neurologist Dr. Tilly Edinger has pointed out: "If man has passed through a Pithecanthropus phase, the evolution of his brain has been unique, not only in its result but also in its tempo. . . . Enlargement of the cerebral hemispheres by 50 per cent seems to have taken place, speaking geologically, within an instant, and without having been accompanied by any major increase in body size."[19]

One reason why the doctrine of human evolution is connected to our nerves is that it is part of the intellectual foundation that supports behaviorism, the ruling ideology of the powerful social sciences. The behaviorists discount the inherent structure of the organism in their stimulus-response formulation, and, therefore, they assume that language and mathematics developed simply because the man-ape carried his fist-hatchet in his hands, leaving his mouth free for babbling.[20] After a geological epoch of babbling, language ability developed. The naïveté of such reasoning is surprising, but it has not gone by unnoticed, for recent work by Chomsky has begun to challenge with some force the simplicity of the behaviorist argument:

Anyone concerned with the study of human nature and human capacities must somehow come to grips with the fact that all normal humans acquire language, whereas acquisition of even its barest rudiments is quite beyond the capacities of an otherwise intelligent ape— a fact that was emphasized, quite correctly, in Cartesian philosophy. It is widely thought that the extensive modern studies of animal communication challenge this classical view; and it is almost universally taken for granted that there exists a [*sic.* "No?"] problem of explaining the evolution of human language from systems of animal communication. However, a careful look at recent studies of animal communication seems to me to provide little support for these assumptions. Rather, these studies simply bring out even more clearly the extent to which human language appears to be a unique phenomenon, without a significant analogue in the animal world. . . .

In fact, the processes by which the human mind achieved its present stage of complexity and its particular form of innate organization are a total mystery, as much so as the analogous questions about the physical or mental organization of any other complex organism. It is perfectly safe to attribute this development to "natural selection," so long as we realize that there is no substance to this assertion, that it amounts to nothing more than a belief that there is some naturalistic explanation for these phenomena.[21]

The Darwinian theory of human evolution by natural selection, which triumphed in the nineteenth and early twentieth centuries, may fall apart into newly structured pieces in the twentieth and early twenty-first centuries. Such an intellectual event would bring about the most overwwhelming and profound changes in the intellectual's world view, and it is precisely this kind of intellectual event that Herman Kahn fails to take into account in his simple projections for international finance in the year 2000.

2. THE PROBLEM OF "THE PRIMITIVE"

The questionable nature of the classic theory of evolution is not a self-contained problem, for the questions branch out in all directions. One immediate problem is the shakiness of the more recent cultural evolution of "primitive" man into the scientific man of Western civilization. During the years in which the countries of Western Europe were busy colonizing the rest of the world, it was irresistibly attractive to them to feel that they were bringing civilization and Christianity to the dumb heathen. The rest of the world was shrouded in animism, magic, and superstition, but England, the nation of Newton, was the bringer of light to the fallen world. So it was very easy for Frazer to construct a scheme of cultural evolution from magic to science and to claim that myth and ritual were simply part of the baggage of men who did not have science.

Frazer was, of course, a victim of the "myth" of his own culture and time, and it remains one of the most intriguing problems of intellectual history to uncover just how the liberals of the Industrial Revolution were able to hide the fact that myth played a great part in the history of science as advanced by such men as Kepler, Descartes, Pascal, and Newton. Had the mystical and Pythagorean nature of pure science not been vigorously suppressed in favor of a scientized political ideology, men like Tennyson might not have had to tear themselves apart over the supposed conflict between visionary experience and reason. But the age demanded an ideology fit for the requirements of an expanding empire, and so the finer distinctions were pushed out of the public mind. Ideology remained subservient to economics, and capitalist and socialist alike structured history into neat schematic progressions: from primitive communism to feudalism to capitalism to socialism, and from manna and animism to polytheism to monotheism to science. Europe claimed monotheism as its own Judeo-Christian heritage and closed its eyes to the fact that monotheism was universal. Before Clive came to India, Brahma was the One unspeakable behind all the gods; before Cortéz came to Mexico, Ometeotl was the one God that generated the many gods. Blind to the monotheism of others, it was no wonder that the Europeans were blind to their own polytheism, for the Catholic had his hagiography of saints for immediate tasks, just as, before him, the ancient Hebrew had Jahweh, but still recited the appropriate Canaanite fertility spell at the planting of his fields.

Evolutionary schemes are hard to do without, if only for the reason that those who construct them always stand on top of them to look down on the conditions that made them what they are. Morgan's scheme of Savagery, Barbarism, and Civilization was attractive to Engels, but now it has outgrown its usefulness. Barbarians built Stonehenge. And as the works of Lévi-Strauss have shown with less obvious cases of mathematical ability, the complexity of "primitive" thinking is impressive. There may indeed be a "mythopoeic mentality," but it is not restricted to precivilized man, but is to be found in geniuses as different as Boehme, Kepler, Blake, Yeats, Wagner, Heisenberg, and that student of Boehme's theory of action and reaction, Isaac Newton. Myth is not an early level of human development, but an imaginative description of reality in which the known is related to the unknown through a system of correspondences in which mind and matter, self, society, and cosmos are integrally expressed in an esoteric language of poetry and number which is itself a performance of the realty it seeks to describe. Myth expresses the deep correspondence between "the universal grammar" of the mind and the universal grammar of events in space-time. A hunk of words does not create a language, and a hunk of matter does not create a cosmos. The structures by which and through which man realizes the intellectual resonance between himself and the universe of which he is a part are his mathematical, musical, and verbal creations. Mediating between Nous and Cosmos is the Logos.

If, then, myth is a positive and creative form of thought that can be present in the most scientific minds, what are we to do with the loss of neatness we find when we abandon the old evolution from myth to science? The Marxist view of history, as articulately presented by archaeologists like V. Gordon Childe, is an elegantly simple and comfortable scheme. We lose a great deal of clarity if we throw it out. But if we take anthropology seriously and accept the fact that there are no such things as primitives, then we pull a thread out of the seam of history and the whole thing begins to come apart.

Perhaps we are now in a historical situation that is analogous to one encountered before in physics. If one is interested in Newtonian problems, then there is nothing as elegant as the formulations of the Newtonian mechanics. However, one small feature of the environment must go unexplained in Newtonian terms: namely, the perihelion of Mercury. To answer this question, one has to enlarge the scope of his conception, and in this case an Einsteinian conception is the answer. But the Einsteinian conception does not negate the previous Newtonian formulation; each system has its own appropriate order of elucidation.

Perhaps it is much the same with history now: if within the period from the neolithic revolution to the twentieth century, one is interested in the relation of economic change and ideological transformation, then the Marxist formulation has a very high order of elucidation. However, a few small features of the environment go unexplained: namely, the mathematical sophistication of neolithic cultures and the cultural evolution of "the primitive." To answer these questions, one has to enlarge his conception beyond the Marxist frame of historical reference. One explanation is that the cataclysmic theory of history is not absurd. There are intelligent primitives because they are not the crude beginning of something, but the fragmentary remains of something else: the detritus of a "Lost World," as the Marxist anthropologist Lévi-Strauss calls it.[22] He does not, of course, invoke the legends of the lost continent of Atlantis (as the first historian of the New World, Oviedo, did in 1550), for Lévi-Strauss is willing to rest with the unknown and has no desire, as Whitehead once said, "to obscure the inherent darkness of the subject," but he does leave things behind for others to pick up. One can only wonder why the Nambikwara, who live deep in the jungles of the Amazon, begin the legends of the tribe with a story of the great flood that destroyed most of humanity.

We do not know the answers yet, but I think some

of the old questions are going to drop as we let go of the illusions that make them necessary. At the moment we are still ignorant enough to think that there are no problems with the commonly accepted narrative of history; and that is an impediment to further knowledge that should be removed. It is difficult to move on when our ignorance is so comfortable and our intuition is warning us that the new knowledge will unsettle our established post-industrial culture. And so it will be only those who are uncomfortable with our established postindustrial culture who will get up to go and see what is outside the air-conditioned, acoustically tiled, and fluorescently lit container our civilization has chosen to end up in.

Some of those who are getting up to go and see are insane, some of them are hippie members of UFO cargo cults, some of them are failures in the status quo, some of them are the radical Catholics who were never at home in the bourgeois culture of "the Protestant Ethic and the Spirit of Capitalism," some of them are revolutionaries who simply like destroying things for the sake of destruction, and some of them are the original thinkers upon whom scientific knowledge depends. Some of those who are not getting up to go and see are sane, some of them are failures in the status quo who identify with their superiors to disguise their failure, some of them are the bourgeois Protestant industrialists who cannot leave because the triumph of the system is what they struggled so long to achieve, some of them are important people who like exercising power for the sake of power, and some of them are the unoriginal

thinkers who maintain the past knowledge upon
which all science depends. We are approaching a
point at which we will have to choose, and the choice
will be hard, but it will be good, for the choice will
tell us, in an almost instinctive act, exactly where
we are.

3. THE PROBLEM OF THE NEOLITHIC AND URBAN REVOLUTIONS

Historians speak of the four great economic revolutions in human culture: the neolithic, urban, industrial, and scientific.[23] In the four-part model I
presented in Chapter 4, I focused not so much on
economic revolutions as economies: hunting, agricultural, industrial, and scientific. In this way I was
able to avoid the traditional distinction between neolithic and urban societies. It was the great Marxist
archaeologist V. Gordon Childe who gave us the
term "the urban revolution,"[24] but recent excavations
have undermined the usefulness of the concept. The
neolithic settlement of Çatal Hüyük in Anatolia
(6500 B.C.) is a town of some thirty-two acres that
shows evidence of luxury items, a developed obsidian
trade with Jericho, and suggestions of internal sexual-
religious class stratification.[25] Such a town is well
advanced on the road to urbanization, so there seems
little reason to isolate the Uruk phase of Mesopotamia some three millennia later to call it "the urban
revolution." And if there is trouble encountered with
this label, there is just as much trouble with the
other label, "the neolithic revolution." By the traditional terms of European archaeology, we must

ignore the highly advanced astronomy, mathematics, and architectural engineering of the Mesoamerican civilizations to call them neolithic because they did not make use of metal tools or the wheel, even though they give brilliant evidence of having done just fine without them.

The concepts of the neolithic and urban "revolutions" are ethnocentric projections of Childe's Marxist belief in dialectical materialism, and they represent what Whitehead would call "misplaced concreteness." There are simply no points in history where we can place such pseudo events in the way we can pinpoint the Industrial Revolution in eighteenth-century Great Britain. The urban revolution is simply an intensification of agricultural society, an intensification in which literacy reinforces the already emerging social stratification of specialists. Specialists must have painted the murals in Lascaux in 12,000 B.C., and there is evidence of continuity in cave art from Lascaux to the upper-paleolithic in Anatolia near Çatal Hüyük. By 6500 B.C. at Çatal Hüyük, the cave art has been transferred to man-made walls and the naturalistic style has been replaced by a stylized iconography, an iconography that is probably an early form of writing for the sacerdotal class. From image to icon is part of a chain of rediscovery that moves on from icon to ideogram or sign, until finally a more abstract form of syllabic writing is achieved. The process is so gradual that the dramatic celebration of pseudo events like the urban revolution tends more to obscure than clarify.

But chronology is not the only problem with Childe's classification, for the very notion of an "urban" civilization is dubious when we have to consider the ceremonial centers of Old Kingdom Egypt or early formative Mesoamerica. Our schemes of history tell us more about ourselves than they do of the past, and even the bland term "formative" has built into it a notion of linear progress. This linear vision is certainly being strained under the weight of Coe's recent finds at San Lorenzo Tenochtitlán:

> Most archaeologists do not believe, as did Sahagún's old men, that the Olmec came from across the Atlantic, or even the Pacific, but the ultimate origins of this first New World Civilization remain in doubt. If their civilization had never been discovered, the "steady evolution" model for the rise of civilization—from gradually cumulative steps toward man's control of his environment and its resources—would look valid. Unfortunately, present evidence indicates that the Olmec appeared upon the scene as an already evolved culture by 1200 B.C.[26]

So we are faced with one sort of evolution in the Old World, a gradual one, and a rapid impositional development in the New World. All of which make historical concepts like neolithic, mesolithic, and chalcolithic appear to be nothing more than regionalisms useful only for describing stratigraphic sequences in restricted areas.

Nevertheless, in eliminating the distinction between neolithic and urban civilizations, we still encounter what Lévi-Strauss calls "the neolithic paradox." Why, when the agricultural transformation of hunting society introduced so many fantastic changes, did it take so long to advance to an industrial civilization?

Neolithic, or early historical, man was therefore the heir of a long scientific tradition. However, had he, as well as all his predecesesors, been inspired by exactly the same spirit as that of our own time, it would be impossible to understand how he could have come to a halt and how several thousand years of stagnation have intervened between the neolithic revolution and modern science like a level plain between ascents. There is only one solution to the paradox, namely, that there are two distinct modes of scientific thought. These are certainly not a function of different stages of development of the human mind but rather two strategic levels at which nature is accessible to scientific inquiry: one roughly adapted to that of perception and the imagination: the other at a remove from it. It is as if the necessary connections which are the object of all science, neolithic or modern, could be arrived at by two different routes, one very close to, and the other more remote from, sensible intuition.[27]

Since "neolithic" and "modern" are not sufficiently descriptive, I would prefer to call the former "Pythagorean science" and the latter "industrial science." Each is the mirror opposite of the other and possesses its own virtues and vices in which *areté* and *hamartia* are one and inseparable. Both sciences are equal if different; the Mayas or Olmecs are not our inferiors because they did not use the wheel. From the pyramids of Egypt to the megaliths of Newgrange, Stonehenge, Mexico, Peru, and Easter Island, ancient man and his Pythagorean science could do things we with our very different industrial science cannot understand. From the Marxist's linear vision of history, these cultures are primitive ones in which what little science they possess is contaminated by religion and superstition. Childe is unequivocal in his judgment: "It is quite obvious that science did not, and could not, spring directly from either magic or religion. We have shown in detail that it originated in, and was at first identical with, the practical crafts. In so far as a craft like that of healing or astronomy was annexed to religion it was sterilized of scientific value."[28]

Now that the internal contradictions of our own industrial science are becoming painfully visible ecologically, we can no longer share that easy confidence in technological progress that filled Professor Childe in 1936. The retardation of progress can come from any entrenched institution, religion, education, or the military. In the cases of Mesopotamia and Mesoamerica, the theocratic polities were followed by the militaristic states that deflected the remote high culture of the astronomically minded elite to more immediate concerns. Since the ceremonial burial of chieftains or Pharaohs requires the withdrawal of valuable materials from the market to the tomb, as Childe points out, there is less opportunity given to expand the base of the market through a growing class of merchants, producers, and consumers. In the specific case of Mesoamerica, whenever the merchant class of Pochtecas advanced to sufficient wealth to threaten the power of the warrior caste, it was robbed of it. Now that militarism is once again deflecting civilized resources into massive armaments, perhaps we can understand how the learned of past cultures were perverted to warlike programs. We were fortunate in that we could not pervert our middle classes into militarism until *after* they had manned the Industrial Revolution (presuming that this revolution proves to be an ultimately good thing). In the cases of Mesopotamia and Mesoamerica, the societies went directly from theocratic feudalism to unbridled militarism. An industrial revolution did not occur in the classic civilizations simply because that revolution was the product of a whole nexus of causes, and that nexus was absent from history until 1760.

If we begin to look at the subject matter of archaeology free of the linear grid of progress and cultural evolution, the old familiar map of history becomes a more mysterious landscape. In the archaeology of the New World one of the most mysterious features of the landscape is that of Olmec culture. The Olmecs are the earliest civilization in Mesoamerica, but they appear with an already developed calendrical system, mathematics, and the technological ability to move hundreds of thousands of tons of material to create the artificial lagoons and mounds of San Lorenzo Tenochtitlán. If accounting for San Lorenzo seems a problem, it is compounded when we consider the other Olmec site of La Venta. Here at this 800 B.C. site are engravings and statues of Negro faces, Oriental faces, Mayan faces, and Semitic faces with perfectly aquiline noses; in some cases the faces have false beards. The colossal negroid heads weigh twenty tons or more and are found on an island, but the rock from which they are quarried comes from mountains seventy kilometers away. Here one should keep in mind that the wheel is known not to have been used, except in children's toys. "The sheer amount of work done by the Olmec, for instance, staggers the imagination.

Similarly, the huge pyramids of Egypt were erected at the beginning of the Nile civilization, not later."[29]

Because "religious fanatics" have plagued Meso-american studies from the beginning, "responsible scholars" have had to shut out all the noise of the lost tribes of Israel and the lost continent of Atlantis, so it is not surprising that Professor Michael Coe, Chairman of the Department of Anthropology at Yale, chooses the imaginative strategy of quoting the old codices without committing himself to their historical validity:

A key piece of data is the memory that the Mexican peoples had of their past, not only of the few centuries before the Spanish Conquest, but of much more distant times. One such account recorded in the Náhuatl language by Father Sahagún opens with, "Behold the story which the old people told," and continues with the legendary arrival of the ancestors of the Mexican people from across the water. Making a landing in what is now Northern Veracruz, they followed the coast line south. At last they came to a place called Tamoanchán. Among them were wise old men who had all the "writings, the books, the paintings" in their possession; then one day they left Tamoanchán carrying these and an image of their god with them. The people left behind were desolate, but four of the old men who had been left behind counseled together and decided to carry on the torch of civilization by themselves.[30]

There is no evidence that the Olmecs came from Europe or Africa, and the Atlantis hypothesis is only entertained at the risk of one's professional reputation. If the successful attack on Velikovsky's publishers did nothing else, it pointed out to the unwary just what kind of modern punishments were avail-

able for modern heresies. So it is not surprising that
Professor Coe teasingly suggests and then coquet-
tishly withdraws from the implications of Sahagún,
just as Lévi-Strauss did before him in his discussion
of "The Lost World." And yet there it is: the same
story keeps cropping up in various sources:

> There they were then, in great number, the black men
> and the white men, men of many classes, men of many
> tongues, that it was wonderful to hear them. . . . In
> this manner, then, came about the disappearance and
> end of Balam-Quitzé, Balam-Acab, Mahucutah, and
> Iqui-Balam, the first men who came there from the
> other side of the sea, where the sun rises.[31]

> Some of the old people of Yucatán say that they
> heard from their ancestors that this land was occupied
> by a race of people, who came from the East and whom
> God had delivered by opening twelve paths through the
> seas.[32]

> "See," said Sótuknang, "I have washed away even
> the footprints of your Emergence; the stepping-stones
> which I left for you [islands]. Down on the bottom of
> the sea lie all the proud cities, the flying *pátuwvotas,* and
> the worldly treasures corrupted with evil, and those
> people who found no time to sing praises to the Creator
> from the tops of their hills. But the day will come, if
> you preserve the memory and the meaning of your
> Emergence, when these stepping-stones will emerge
> again to prove the truth you speak.[33]

One is free to treat myth as lightly as one would
a rumor, and if one has inherited the positivism of
the nineteenth century in its new behavioral science
form, he is quite likely to dismiss the sources (and
the racial faces at La Venta) as scraps for vulgar

amateurs. But myth is not rumor; in a literate society, rumors change from teller to teller because the memory of civilization is safely stored in the libraries; but in preliterate societies (or should we say post-literate societies?) The racial history is stored in the oral legends and chronicles, and these are endowed with such sacredness that one would never dream of acting like a modern artist who changes whatever pleases his own taste. In a religious society, myth tells the people who they are, and where they come from; to change the myth is to run the risk of becoming lost in the most profound ontological sense. It is no wonder that the Maya Indians were inconsolable, beyond any expectation that Bishop de Landa had before he started, when they saw their painted books going up in flames in the good bishop's *auto-da-fé*.

But Bishop de Landa was not the only one guilty of trying to wipe out all knowledge of the past. In good Stalinist fashion, "King Itzcóatl ordered the ancient codices to be burned so that a new official version of Aztec history could be established."[34] Whenever it has suited his ideological purposes, man has scrupulously destroyed or ignored the record of the past so that its tragedies could not interfere with progress and the ambitions of the present. Voltaire knew what he was talking about when he said: "History is the lie commonly agreed upon." Our view of the past is a fiction we create to rationalize our position of power in the present, and our view of the future is simply a magnification of our present; and that is as true of Herman Kahn as it is of King Itzcóatl. But, perhaps, the Aztec king was more honest, at least with himself, for he knew what he was doing and why. Today's social scientists are more often the prisoners of their own fictions.

If man has tried very hard to destroy or discredit his knowledge of the past, then it is little wonder that there can be vast gaps in which civilizations could exist without our officially approved knowledge. If so brilliant a man as David Hume could claim, in his history of England, that no civilization existed in Ireland before the Normans conquered it (when, in fact, it was Irish scholars Charlemagne called upon when he wished to end the Dark Ages and found the Holy Roman Empire), why should we think that we are now immune to the same ethnocentric ignorance and blindness? Consciously or unconsciously, most of our Mesoamerican historians avoid the pieces of information that would unsettlle their world view. The earlier American archaeologists thought that their Mexican colleagues were being chauvinistic in claiming an early date for the Olmecs, but their argument showed their own preconceptions, for they felt that nothing so developed could be so old. In the end, the remains proved to be far older than anyone had expected, and this discovery has only compounded the problems in explaining Olmec culture.

To be sympathetic with the Americans, one always has to bear in mind that archaeologists are always plagued with newspapermen trying to get flashy copy on lost worlds who are quite willing to embarrass the scholar by mishandling the information for effect. Inevitably, the scholar vows never to make the same mistake again and to reserve his finds for the most narrowly published scholarly journals. Unfortunately, this strategy of self-defense only encourages a rigidity against all unaccepted and unorthodox theories. Between the cracked-open minds of the enthusiasts of lost tribes, lost continents, and flying saucers and the firmly shut minds of the scholars, it is very difficult to find a healthy way of using one's head. It is only too easy to make fun of the academic mentality, but when one leaves the disciplined mentality of the professional behind, he finds himself with all space to move around in, and a lot of wild things move around in the space of the unknown.

For example, a Mixtec Indian told me at Monte Albán that a date of 1500 B.C. for the site was thrown out because it was so early as to be absurd. Since that seemed likely enough, I began to move toward his position, and then the price tag for affiliation came up. He went on to say that the sarcophagus on the Temple of Inscriptions at Palenque was a Mayan vision of a space ship, that the gods who gathered at Teotihuacán to initiate the Fifth World (one that is supposed to end in earthquakes by 2011) were really extraterrestrials, the "Sons of God" mentioned in the Bible, and that the helmet on the negroid Olmec heads was really a space pilot's headpiece. The last point really appealed to my sense of irony, for I had a vision of tall, elegant Watusis disembarking from a saucer on the lawn of the White House just after a George Wallace had been elected. It would provide a poetic finish for the last administration of the Great White Race that had enslaved the Negroes, massacred the Indians, and imprisoned the American-Japanese. The other listeners standing by were fascinated at his account of how "the gods" were really beings from another planet, and a woman from Chicago told us how her sci-fi son believed earth to have been colonized from Venus (which is an old Annie Besant, Theosophical doctrine in a new vessel). And so the whole cargo cult story was a great success, which, no doubt, was one good reason the Indian made it a practice.

The double-bind was as true of scholarship as of politics: one purchased discipline at a cost of imagination; one purchased imagination at a cost of discipline; a disciplined imagination was a contradiction in terms. If one twisted his head around in the position recommended by the Mixtec Indian (and some new books[35]) to entertain the view that primitives aren't primitive and that when they say that the gods came out of the sky bringing the arts of civilization, we are to take them literally, then the university, which Plato founded, has ended up in Plato's cave. It is much easier to hold onto the idea of the "cargo cult," and to see the followers as people suffering from the stress of a highly complex, pluralistic society that no longer provides the mythic comforts of a religious society.[36] For a person like myself, a cultural historian working within a university, it becomes much simpler to follow Plato and Oviedo and identify the gods with the superior technology as the denizens of the lost continent of Atlantis. The two theories, of course, are not mutually exclusive, and many of the uneducated have already made up their minds in favor of the gods, which only forces the professors back to protect themselves from their eager sci-fi, hippie students. As the mind of the university hardens, and the minds of the dropouts loosen almost to the point of coming apart, one will be able to appreciate why the ancients believed in keeping knowledge as a secret mystery for the initiate.

But it is just this secret, conspiratorial, and eso-teric nature of the alternate vision of history that is most maddening. The more one looks, the more he finds; and even in not looking his newly sensitized eyes stop at things he would never have noticed before. The pattern spreads everywhere around him like a Trystero system, for Plato, Oviedo, and the Mexican codices are not the only ones that make reference to Atlantis. The ancient Irish *Book of Invasions* and the voyage poems, the *Imramha,* mention the mysterious Islands of the West, and the *Book of Invasions* describes the battles of these western Fomorians with the peoples of Europe. In the *Voyage of Bran* the hero sails out to the West to the Happy Isles; on his return from his mysterious adventure in that strange land, he comes back to Ireland to find that he is three hundred years older in Ireland, and that the *Voyage of Bran* is now one of their ancient legends. I could never understand, in the ordinary terms of literary criticism, what the relativistic time-shift was doing in an eighth-century poem—a poem that as an oral folk tale goes even further back to an unknown past. But if history is reversed so that the further back we go, *the more advanced* things become, then what is magic in a folk tale is simply what was once science in the vanished high culture.

This is not as absurd as it may seem if one stops to think of the lacunae in historical time. Five hundred years ago Columbus crossed the ocean in a bloated rowboat and now we are walking on the moon. In historical reckoning five hundred years is often the carbon-14 increment of plus or minus 250 years, so there are many places in history where we leap over centuries to the next fact simply because we have nothing to fill up the space. A civilization could have arisen in 10,500 B.C., climaxed in 10,000, and destroyed itself by 9500. The missing continent, like the missing particle in physics, would certainly make a lot more sense of Mexico and Peru. When one considers that Plato, the Irish legends, and the Mexican chronicles all place a civilization destroyed by flood in the Atlantic, then M. I. Finley's flippant dismissal of "more Atlantis nonsense" becomes more difficult.[37] It is one thing to support a fantasy of history upon the *Timaeus,* and quite another to support it from similar material from three widely separated cultures. Since many civilizations were unbelieved legends until they were uncovered, we cannot be so certain that Atlantis will not follow the example of Schliemann's Troy.

J. V. Luce has recently put together an articulate presentation of the work of the group of scholars trying to prove that the cataclysmic destruction of Minoan Thera circa 1470 B.C. is the historical core of Plato's Atlantean myth.[38] The argument is a reasonable one, and were there no other material available to us, it would be fairly convincing. However, Atlantis in the Aegean nine hundred years before Solon's time and Atlantis in the Atlantic nine thousand years before Solon's time are not the mutually exclusive theories that Luce seems to think they are. Most myths are as stratified as archaeological ruins, for in "the mythopoeic mentality" a historical event is often only another performance of the mythic, archetypal pattern. There is not just one Quetzalcoatl. For years scholars confused Ca Acatl Tepolitzin Quetzalcoatl and the fall of Tula with the more ancient Quetzalcoatl and the fall of Tollan, just as, much later, the Aztecs associated the fall of their own Tenochtitlán with the newly arrived Quetzalcoatl-Cortéz. Siimilarly, when Padraic Pearse died in Dublin in 1916, he envisioned himself as the sacrificial hero of pagan Ireland, Cuchulain. If Ireland had been still pagan in 1916, Pearse's apotheosis in death would have involved the new name of Patrick Cuchulain—to the consternation of archaeologists of A.D. 4000, who would be rather hard pressed to separate the figures of Cuchulain, St. Patrick, and Patrick Henry, all collapsed into the single personage of Patrick Henry Pearse. Atlantis is in the Aegean, in the Atlantic, and, perhaps, even in the Lemuria of the Pacific.

Because history is often the performance of myth, our touch must become more delicate if we are not to destroy the most ancient past in our rapid handling of the more comfortably recent past. The positivist's distrust of myth will not vanish overnight, but his cocky assuredness has been undermined by archaeological corroborations of myth all over the world. The work of Nelson Glueck and W. F. Albright in Israel is, perhaps, one of the most outstanding examples:

Eminent names among scholars can be cited for regarding every item of Gen. 11–50 as reflecting late invention, or at least retrojection of events and conditions under the Monarchy into the remote past, about which nothing was thought to have been really known to the writers of later days.

Archaeological discoveries since 1925 have changed all this. Aside from a few die-hards among older scholars, there is scarcely a single biblical historian who has not been impressed by the rapid accumulation of data supporting the substantial historicity of patriarchal tradition.[39]

In the spirit of Albright, Manson Valentine is now trying to confirm the Noachian myth. The story of Noah in the canonical Bible gives little indication of a pre-existing civilization, but in the Book of Enoch or the Midraash there are clearer references to the scraps of the old science that Noah was able to preserve:

A pearl hanging from the ark's roof shone calmly on Noah and his family. When its light paled, he knew that the hours of daylight had come; when it brightened, he knew that night was at hand, and thus never lost count of the Sabbaths. Some say, however, that this light came from a sacred book which the Archangel Raphael gave to Noah, bound in sapphires, and containing all knowledge of the stars, the art of healing and the mastery of demons.[40]

The Sumerians, too, have a myth of deluge and a Noah who is warned by God in advance, but the story of Utnapishtim is not the only Sumerian reference to the antediluvian order. Like the Mexicans, the Sumerians refuse to take the credit for building their cities; they claim that kingship descended before the flood, and that before man lived in the cities, the gods did. The early ruler of a city was not a king, he was an *ensi*, a steward for the absentee landlord who was the god of the city. Only much later, in the secular age, did the king begin to rule in his own right and stopped pretending he was holding the city for the return of its absent god.

Limited by the world view current in their day and accepted as axiomatic truth—that cultural phenomena and historical events came ready-made, "full grown, full blown," on the world scene, since they were planned by the all powerful gods—it probably never occurred to even the most thoughtful and learned of the Sumerian sages that Sumer had once been desolate marshland with but a few scattered settlements and had only gradually come to be a bustling, thriving, and complex community after many generations of struggle and toil in which human will and determination, man-laid plans and experiments, and man-made discoveries and inventions played a predominant role.[41]

One would think that generations of toil would not be ignored and disowned by a people who were intelligent enough to be the creators of "the world's first civilization," but somehow Professor Kramer thinks the Sumerians were intelligent enough to begin history but not intelligent enough to understand what they were doing. Sumer is a poor stoneless place for a neolithic culture to evolve from a peasant community into a full-blown civilization, but it is a very good place to turn the plains and marshes into irrigated farmlands, so that what is a disadvantage on one level of order becomes an advantage on a higher one. In short, Sumer is an ideal place to locate a culture already having the technology necessary for urban life and irrigation agriculture.

Professor Kramer is one of the most distinguished Sumerologists in the world, but, once again, the double-bind condition of life means that he has had to purchase his specialized triumph at a cost of the general knowledge that would call his simplistic ideas of anthropology and comparative religion into question. Consequently, Kramer slips into an outworn argument and speaks condescendingly of the Sumerians as "limited by the world view current in their day." A future historian might well say the same of Professor Kramer. "The sketch of Sumerian history here presented no doubt suffers from the author's particular prejudices, conceits, and shortcomings; but this is the best he can do with the data available in the year 1963." Kramer goes on to describe these data as being "fragmentary, obscure, and elusive." And so no one knows for certain just what the Sumerians meant by the word *dingir,* which Kramer chooses to translate as "god." My Mixtec companion at Monte Albán would, no doubt, rejoicingly claim these gods to be the flying saucer colleagues of the gods of Teotihuacán, or "the Watchers from Heaven" of The Book of Enoch.[42] Since I have never placed my doubting fingers into the side of a flying saucer, I would prefer, while remaining open to all possibilities (including my being just plain wrong about Atlantis), to be much more academic and consider the Sumerians as members of a peasant community who encountered refugees from Atlantis who imposed their culture upon them—much in the same way that the Olmecs seem to have imposed their culture on the indigenous communalistic villages of archaic Mexico.

All in all, when one takes into account the problems that are not honestly faced and questioned in our notions of evolution, primitive culture, and archaeology, he can see that the specialists of what T. S. Kuhn would call "normal science" are retreating from the "anomalies" and burrowing more deeply into the security of minutiae. If one lifts his gaze to take in the whole historical horizon of man, as now only an amateur or a non-specialist can, he can see that once again we are entering an era of scientific revolution with its sudden shift in paradigms.

Therefore, at times of revolution, when the normal-scientific tradition changes, the scientist's perception of his environment must be re-educated—in some familiar situations he must learn to see a new gestalt . . .
Almost always the men who achieve these fundamental inventions of a new paradigm have been either very young or very new to the field whose paradigm they change.[43]

Our present world view is being put under a strain. The keystone of our world structure has not yet been pulled out, but if irrefutable artifacts are in the Bahamas, and if these artifacts are brought to light at a time when our confidence in rational Technological Society is being destroyed by political conflict, ecological catastrophes, and world-wide famines, then the whole arch will come down with a crash as a msytic's prophecies are proved to be accurate.

The liberal humanists dread the collapse of their world structure with some reason, for if progress and materialism have made technology possible by ignoring all the other subtle forces in nature, then the death of materialism will open man up to beasts and demons he has not feared since the Middle Ages. Science often progresses upon ignorant over-simplifications until the simplifications wear out their usefulness and are discarded. Now as the simplifications are indeed wearing out, the young are being accosted by new complexities that they cannot handle. Already the hippie dropouts from our universities and high schools are becoming caught up in black magic, sorcery, and the crudest forms of occultism, and Charles Manson in Los Angeles and the Zodiac killer in San Francisco are showing us what happens when twentieth-century rational and fatuous man fades away. The Pythagorean synthesis of science, religion, and art advocated by Whitehead and Teilhard de Chardin will be angelic, but the cultural transformation of our society will also involve all the subrational returns of the demonic.

The occult is keeping pace with our Technological Society, and when man first circled the moon, the Cabalists in the Near East said that the evil spirits placed there by King Solomon would now come to haunt the earth again: in breaking open the seal of his encasement on earth, man had broken open the universe. In a figurative way, the myth, like all myths, will probably prove to contain a profound truth, for the industrial universities that made the moonshot possible seem to be disintegrating politically at the very moment of their triumph. And though I do not wish to associate the Biblical fundamentalist, Edgar Cayce, with the most demonic of recent occult fascinations, the fact that millions read him is probably a more important event in our culture than the formation of the American Academy of Arts and Sciences' Commission on the Year 2000. But whether Cayce is a prophet of a new age or simply a symptom of our contemporary malaise is at least one thing we will not have to wait for the year 2000 to uncover.

II

The pastoral vision of Kentucky-born Cayce is certainly an antidote to the extreme urbanization of Kahn, but the difficulty with Cayce's apocalypse is that it depends on humanity's being saved by the intervention of nature. Just as man is about to destroy himself with a completely savage technology, nature intervenes, the earth gives out from under his feet, and ancient man is brought back to his senses by the return of his most ancient antagonist. Cayce's apocalypse reveals so perfect a sense of timing that it goes against the grain of our modern skepticism, which suspects the world will end, as Eliot said, not with a bang, but a whimper. It seems now more likely that color TV's will keep man happy in his cell as the species slowly deteriorates. If one adopts Cayce's vision, he has only to sit and wait for cataclysms to bring man to a primordial consciousness of himself, and while he waits, he grows farther away from humanity and its contemporary consciousness.

When one believes in an alternate vision of history, whether it is Atlantean, Christian, or cargo cult, he is stepping outside the city to see a pastoral vision in which the office buildings and the universities do not obscure the archaic stars. All through history, from Abraham to Mao, prophets have left the city behind them to insist upon a vision of things greater than they are; but in the double nature of all phenomena, the abandoning of the city for the wilderness is also the pattern of madness: the psychotic leaves the social structure of sanity. From the psychotic's point of view, one could paraphrase Voltaire to say that sanity is the lie commonly agreed upon. Those left behind in the city define themselves as responsible and sane and see the wanderer as a madman. The wanderer defines himself as the only sane person in a city of the insane and walks out in search of other possibilities. All history seems to pulse in this rhythm of urban views and pastoral visions, and the conflict between them is the theme of one of the novels of another prophet of the year 2000, Arthur C. Clarke.

The religious mythology of Cayce, widespread as it is, is still a small ripple compared to the movement of science fiction. For people of my age, the visions of Arthur C. Clarke are what the novels of H. G. Wells were to another generation. Scores of students I have met at Cal Tech and M.I.T. have had their scientific imaginations profoundly touched by the atheistic mysticism of Clarke. If, as Teilhard de Chardin suggests, art, religion, and science are to become one in the coming age of "the planetisation of mankind," then the unique synthesis is probably more characterized by Arthur C. Clarke than by fundamentalist Cayce or scientifically illiterate hippies.

The City and the Stars is Clarke's version of the pastoral and urban conflict in human history. Diaspar is a city of a future a billion years hence, but really, as in most such projections, as McLuhan has noted, it is a city that is only an idealized version of the present. Diaspar is a triumph of technology, closed in upon itself under a huge dome, its every function, from the moving sidewalks to the materialization devices that create one's every need, is taken care of by an enormous computer. In this perfect city man is not born of woman, but he emerges fully grown from the Hall of Creation to begin a life of thousands of years. After the fullness of millennia, man returns to his source; his atoms and his program are all undone for a time until, once again, he is reincarnated for another existence. But once in a million times or so, a man emerges from the Hall of Creation who is not a repeated version of those who lived before. Alvin, the hero of the novel, is just such a "unique."

Alvin shows his uniqueness by being uneasy in Zion. A vague unsettledness wears away at him, and while all the others seem to fit perfectly into their technological paradise, Alvin grows restless and wants to know the inconceivable: what is outside Diaspar? Everyone in Diaspar knows that a cosmic war destroyed most of human civilization an aeon ago, and that man, whose empire had once been vast, was forced to retreat from the Terror that came from beyond space to this last island solitude.

All the knowledge of the great men of the past went into making up for the loss of space by creating a city that would defy time and the second law of thermodynamics. The city, and the consciousness of the people inside it, was a perfect sphere; there were no edges, no end and no beginning, for everything curved back upon itself. It was inconceivable to think of an outside; they were so perfectly programmed by the Hall of Creation that the intimation of an outside was enough to undermine the very structure of their consciouness. But Alvin was unique, and his restlessness would not leave him alone until he began his search to find a way out of Diaspar. As Alvin begins to think that everything his fellows believe is a myth, he trembles at the thought of just how alien he is. "When such thoughts crossed his mind, it seemed as if the structure of reality trembled for an instant, and that behind the world of the senses he caught a glimpse of another and totally different universe."

In his search for the inconceivable, one person comes to Alvin's aid. Because Diaspar is perfect, the founding scientists knew that its survival would depend on one calculated aberration of absolute perfection, and so they created the office of the Jester and gave him access to the central computer. Aided by the computer, the Jester could harass the perfect citizens in just the right degree of variation from absolute order that would ensure the continuation of the city. The Jester helps Alvin as part of just such a possible harassment, and, therefore, brings him to the central office where he can survey the entire city to look for a way out of the perfect sphere.

But when Alvin succeeds, as he never thought he could, the Jester is horrified that the prank is more terrifyingly real than he could ever imagine. He withdraws from the crisis he has created, scatters his atoms in the Hall of Creation, and sets a return for a time when his error will only be dim history.

But Alvin does not withdraw from the terror of his quest, and like most mythic heroes he finds that it is the terror on this side and not the other that is real. Outside there are no monsters and no unbearable wastes; but outside there is Lys, the other country from which no traveler has ever returned. Appropriately, Lys is the mirror opposite of Diaspar:

> Lys had been little different, in the.early days, from hundreds of other communities. But gradually, over the ages, it developed an independent culture which was one of the highest that mankind had ever known. It was a culture based largely upon the direct use of mental power, and this set it apart from the rest of human society, which came to rely more upon machines.
> Through the aeons, as they advanced along their different roads, the gulf between Lys and the cities widened. It was bridged only in times of great crisis; when the Moon was falling, its destruction was carried out by the scientists of Lys. So also was the defense of Earth against the Invaders.[44]

Lys is natural in all the ways that Diaspar is unnatural. In Lys there are children, and man is still born of woman; in Lys they grow their food and do not synthesize it; in Lys they communicate telepathically and not telegraphically. But the meeting of Lys and Diaspar is no accidental event; it is a moment of human destiny. Through Alvin, the unique, human history is about to begin again after

its long hibernation in the cave of Diaspar. And the
first moment of awakening is to realize that all that
one had thought before was so intensely real was
merely a dream; the history that had pillowed one's
head was completely false. It is a difficult awakening
for Diaspar:

> . . . what they had discovered was so strange that it
> bore scarcely any resemblance to the history which all
> the human race had accepted for a billion years. . . . For
> ages, Man sank into a superstitious yet still scientific
> barbarism during which he distorted history to remove
> his sense of impotence and failure.[45]

The history of Diaspar was a myth; man never
extended his empire to the stars; he was barely at
the edge of his own solar system when the stars
came to him. And because Diaspar's history was a
false myth, change could only be brought about by
a man who walked out of "reality" and came back;
the Jester, who subverted society from within the
system, could only help to keep it strong. Political
rebels like the Jester preserve society, but Messiahs
like Alvin the unique annul it. But Alvin's work as
redeeming savior is not merely to effect the magic
of leaving Diaspar. The full resurrection of human
history requires that man overcome the full effects
of the original fall into Diaspar. If man was to begin
again, the opposites he had kept apart for aeons
would have to be brought back together to create
the new culture in which he could once again claim
his birthright. The novel ends with Diaspar and
Lys moving out of the cities and back toward the
stars.

Clarke's 1953 novel is uncanny in its prophecy,

for his billion-year future seems to be an imaginative description of our present. The United States is Diaspar and the land of the Hopi is Lys. We are the people closed in a culture of machines in which artificial intelligence, artificial organs, and extrauterine birth are promising to give "man" the future he has always dreamed of. The Hopis are the small spiritually and psychically advanced people watching us move toward apocalypse and remembering the prophecies.[46] Some of the people of Diaspar are trying to find the way out, but as they leave the central computer behind them to return to the earth where they can grow simple food, build a culture of consciousness, and make a sacrament out of the sexuality of their own bodies, they are only moving into the suburbs of Diaspar where the technological pollution of earth is matched by the internal technological pollution of their minds. For the Hopis, it makes no sense to leave Los Angeles in the body and hold it tightly in the mind; for them the only way out of Diaspar is through the door at the top of the head.

Clarke is a prophet, but his prophecy is not so much prediction as the imaginative description of the implications of the present. One part of mankind wishes to take us into rockets, computers, and a cultural unity that comes from computerized medicine, computerized music, poetry, and film, and cybernetic organisms in which the education of the mind is achieved by hooking up the cells of the brain directly to teaching machines. The other part of mankind is struggling to develop consciousnes so as to obviate the need for machines. If one has *pratyahara* (yogic control of the senses), he has no need of drugs; if one has *kriya* (control of the central nervous system), he has no need of computers; if one has *samadhi* (cosmic consciousness), he has no need of moon rockets; for it is the characteristic of an infinite space that all the points are equidistant from one another, and so one does not have to *get* anywhere if he is at his own center. Yet in 1970 there is no doubt that the gyre of Diaspar is at its widest expansion, and that the gyre of Lys is merely as small as the eye of a needle.

> *All the stream that's roaring by*
> *Came out of a needle's eye;*
> *Things unborn, things that are gone,*
> *From needle's eye still goad it on.*[47]

An apocalyptic visionary like Yeats would say that at the time one gyre is tiniest in the magnitude of the other is just that time when things are polarized to extremes and man and God fight over what remains between them. "Now his wars on God begin/ At stroke of midnight God shall win." But for an atheistic visionary like Clarke, it is not man and God who fight, but man, his artificial machines, and the physical nature and stellar beings who remain beyond them. It is this ultimate transforming conflict that is the theme of Clarke's novel and film, *2001: A Space Odyssey,* and it was with this work that Clarke's fame grew beyond the circle of his science fiction followers to his present popularity.

One thing that unites Edgar Cayce and Arthur C. Clarke is the contention that human evolution is not the result of a single, natural, uninterrupted process. In the case of Cayce it was the children of Lilith who fell into bestiality by projecting themselves into sexual bodies, and it was the children of Adam who took on physical form to help their fallen brothers back out of matter:

(Of the souls which God created—and He created all souls in the beginning; none has been made since —only a comparatively few have come into the experience of the solar system, though many have gone through or are going through a similar entanglement in other systems.)

A way of escape for the souls which were entangled in matter was prepared. A form was chosen to be a vehicle for the soul on earth, and the way was made for souls to enter earth and experience it as part of their cycle. Of the forms already existing on earth one of the anthropoid apes most nearly approached the necessary pattern. Souls descended on these apes—hovering above and about them rather than inhabiting them— and influenced them to move toward a different goal from the simple one they had been pursuing. They came down out of the trees, built fires, made tools, lived in communities, and began to communicate with each other. Swiftly, even as man measures time, they lost their animal look, shed bodily hair, and took on refinements of manner and habit.

All this was done by the souls, working through the glands, until the body of the ape was an objectification —in the third dimension of the solar system—of the soul that hovered above it. Then the soul descended into the body and earth had a new inhabitant: man.[48]

What is interesting about this description of the origin of man is that it simultaneously affirms the truth of the two contradictory positions of the Biblical fundamentalist and the physical anthropologist, and thereby serves as a marvelous demonstration of Buddhist logic. In the Structuralist school of myth analysis, Lévi-Strauss contends that one must take into account every variation of a myth, no matter how late or artificial the variant may be. In a study of the Oedipus myth, Freud's theories become one variation of the myth to be set alongside that of Sophocles. Now if we take Edgar Cayce's version of the myth of the fall of man, put it alongside those of C. S. Lewis, Arthur C. Clarke, and, say, the ancient Mexican myth, we will come up with a core-structure that represents the universal myth of human nature. In the case of the Mexican myth, the story runs that in the island of Aztlán, man descended the sacred tree to come down into earth. The Cabalistic tree with its lights, the Indian spinal column tree with its chakras, the Sumerian huluppu tree of Gilgamesh and Innana, the tree of Adam and Eve, is also the ancient Mexican tree.

Out of the split at the top of the skull or cave these two energies, male and female, immortal and at the same time ephemeral in all their palpable manifestations, can come forth. In one hymn the god of fire says:

> *I tie a rope to the sacred tree.*
> *I plait it with eight strands so that I—*
> *a magician—*
> *may descend to the magical house.*[49]

Mythological symbolism is, of course, esoteric in the extreme, and that is why a modern mythic artist like Clarke must find a language and imagery more in keeping with the culture of a technological people. In Clarke's modern myth of the origin of man, beings come from the stars and discover the man-apes, see that they are ripe for a quantum leap in evolution, and decide to influence their development.

How many of those potential heavens and hells are now inhabited, and by what manner of creatures, we have no way of guessing; the very nearest is a million times farther away than Mars or Venus, those still remote goals of the next generation. But the barriers of distance are crumbling; one day we shall meet our equals, or our masters, among the stars.

Men have been slow to face this prospect; some still hope that it may never become reality. Increasing numbers, however, are asking: "Why have such meetings not occurred already, since we ourselves are about to venture into space?"

Why not indeed? Here is one possible answer to that very reasonable question. But please remember: this is only a work of fiction.

The truth, as always, will be far stranger.[50]

Men have not really been so slow to face the prospect, for it is really only the managerial class that has not widely accepted what would constitute a complete reversal of its supremacy. The universal cargo cult takes in multitudes, from Oxford professors like Lewis waiting for Christ to invade, through Clarke and his followers, to the Mixtec Indians, looking at Apollo 11 and remembering their ancient gods from the sky. And even the Russians have held conferences on extraterrestrial civilizations and begun to wait, with Mick Jagger, "for something to come out of somewhere." A few Rusian heretics have even dared to doubt dialectical materialism in a complete re-visioning of the nature of historical reality:

Yu. Krasovsky opens with references to a couple of instances of individuals casting doubt on the strictly materialistic bias of Marxism-Leninism. From there he moves into a lengthy discussion and criticism of the "hypothesis" of V. K. Zaitsev, lecturer in philology at Minsk University. This theory assumes some extra-terrestrial civilization which has been "programming" the history of mankind on earth in more or less direct ways. Manifestations of this are suggested to be angels, appear-ances of gods on earth, visions, etc. It seems that this theory was weighed and condemned by a scientific com-mission of Leningrad State University as long ago as 1962, but has now reappeared in "improved" form in two journals. Krasovsky criticizes Zaitsev for allowing himself to be led into baseless speculations and for fail-ing to see that his hypothesis admits the supernatural to a degree that is no less harmful than the Christian faith itself. He condemns the theory because, like religion, it undermines the role of man and his ability to change his circumstances. He criticizes the journals in question for printing these articles.[51]

If Marx stood Hegel on his head, it would seem that Zaitsev is standing anthropology on its head to make the anthropologists primitives, and the cargo cult natives savants of extraterrestrial cultures.

Looking at Kubrick's film version of Clarke's story of the programming of human history, one almost has to accept the theory of extraterrestrial intervention in human evolution. Watching the film's Australopithecinae at work, it is almost impossible to conceive of their developing a language without radical alteration. The hypothesis of intervention seems almost as unbelievable as the hypothesis of evolution to Homo Sapiens. It is ironic that the acting of the apes, which is intended to make evolu-tion seem all the more believable, only succeeds in making it seem incredible: thus we are prepared to accept the even more incredible arrival of the star beings.

But that is not the only irony in Kubrick's sardonic way of looking at things. The film itself is the perfect American irony: a gadget-filled, special-effects ode to technology that is at once a requiem to all technology. The very movie that dazzles us with all its tricks is the movie that shows how trivial all these toys are when set upon the cosmic scale. Man has triumphed in conquering the moon, but in order to do so he has had to turn himself into a machine. He has also had to create intelligent machines to keep him company in his escape from earth. But as technological man settles his bases on the moon, he finds that he is not the first to come there. A monolithic artifact of some three million years of age is discovered, and as the sunlight touches it, it emits a signal to Jupiter—an alarm that the man-ape has now escaped his planet.

The astronauts are, of course, shocked to discover that the universe is not their undeveloped country waiting only for its colonial destiny. They are also frightened that they may have triggered an alarm that will bring visitors to do to them what they were about to do to other worlds. All news of the discovery is suppressed. Ostensibly the secrecy is to avoid a culture shock that could panic the earth, but it is obvious from the banality of the bureaucratic lies that the real fear is that proof of extraterrestrial intelligence subverts the technocrats' entire culture of power on earth. The technology with which they have impressed or intimidated the nonscientific mass is threatened if there is anything beyond it. The culture shock is not to the ignorant devotees of UFO's but to the technologists themselves, and so the government must lie because the truth is not in its self-interest. As Marx has said: "The ruling ideas are the ideas of the ruling class."

So complete is their lie that even the mission that is sent to Jupiter to trace the signal knows nothing of its true purpose. Only Hal, the 9000 series computer, knows the real nature of the mission, but he is forced to conceal it from the crew. To be programmed always to tell the truth, but never to reveal the true nature of the mission, however, creates a conflict in the basic categories of the computer's program. The secret becomes an intolerable category violation, and Hal, forced to live human lies, begins to go awry as the stress from this "cognitive dissonance" builds up. At last the infallible 9000 series computer makes a mistake in front of his fallible human companions, and now poor Hal's very identity is being eroded. When he overhears how his disturbed crew members intend to disconnect him, his identity shatters completely in a psychotic seizure in which he, the perfect computer, attempts to rid the ship of the humans whom he now sees as the source of imperfection and contradiction in an otherwise perfect mission.

Hal is correct about humans as the source of his internal contradictions, but those responsible for his programmed "Lie and tell the truth" are not the victims at hand. As Hal and the ship's captain come into mortal combat, there is an exchange of opposites in which the computer becomes human and the astronaut becomes a deadly machine with one purpose: to disconnect Hal. It is a fitting irony: at the very edge of our human history, man and machine fight out their natures, and man only barely succeeds in conquering the machines that have made his space flight possible. But by the time he has won, "man" is beginning to approach his end.

Having disconnected Hal, Bowman, the captain, settles back to sit out the long journey to Japetus, the moon of Jupiter. He tries to while away his time in reading and listening to tapes, but, from Clarke's point of view, the culture of Homo Sapiens is not a very enlightening one.

At first, needing the companionship of the human voice, he had listened to classical plays—especially the works of Shaw, Ibsen, and Shakespeare—or poetry readings from *Discovery*'s enormous library of recorded sounds. The problems they dealt with, however, seemed so remote, or so easily resolved with a little common sense, that after a while he lost patience with them.[52]

But Bowman's fidgeting with antique knowledge does not have to last forever; finally he comes to Japetus and sets out to explore it in the mother ship's smaller shuttle craft. There he finds a colossal version of the monolith that had marked the turning points in the path of man's evolution. As he approaches it, he finds that it is really a hole in space filled with the light of another universe. Bowman radios back his final words, and like the World War II pilot who, before he disappeared into the Bermuda Triangle, radioed back: "Where are we? It looks like the world rolled over . . ." his words are to become equally immortal back on earth: "The thing's hollow —it goes on forever—and—oh my God! it's full of stars."

Technology is of little use with a race that has

transcended the body, for Bowman takes a voyage to another universe in which the entities "In their ceaseless experimenting . . . had learned to store knowledge in the structure of space itself, and to preserve their thoughts for eternity in frozen lattices of light. They could become creatures of radiation, free at last from the tyranny of matter." The star beings read his mind, settled him down in a motel environment taken from TV programs of earth, and then begin their work on him, as aeons ago they worked upon his ape-man ancestors. Bowman grows old instantly and becomes, on the other side of death, a fetus bound for incarnation on the earth. And a star-transformed man is exactly what the earth is in need of, for now there is indeed panic and sub-orbital weapons are being triggered. But it is a small matter for the mind of the star child to destroy them as a prelude to his second coming to earth.

III

And so it all comes down to the same thing in the end, whether we start with the technological fantasies of Herman Kahn, the mysticism of Edgar Cayce, or the cosmic fictions of Arthur C. Clarke. Western Civilization is drawing to a close in an age of apocalyptic turmoil in which the old species, collectivizing mankind with machines, and the new species, unifying it in consciousness, are in collusion with one another to end what we know as human nature. Western man will no doubt try to prove that he is not merely mud to be shaped into bricks for the dreamers' temples, but even taking the conservative obstinacy of industrial man into account, it would still seem that we are at one of those moments when the whole meaning of nature, self, and civilization is overturned in a re-visioning of history as important as any technological innovation.

Birth is a cry of joy and a scream of pain: the environment that sustained us for a time is now crushing down and pushing us out. But death, too, is a scream of pain and a cry of joy, and so we cannot be certain that we are headed for one and not the other. Birth and death are ultimately confusing; to make sense of them we will have to make our peace with myth.

We will have to come right up to the edge to find out where we are, and who we are. At the edge of history, history itself can no longer help us, and only myth remains equal to reality. What we know is less than what we are, and so the politcs of miracle must be unacceptable to our knowledge to be worthy of our being. *Credo quia absurdum est.* The future is beyond knowing, but the present is beyond belief. We make so much noise with technology that we cannot discover that the stargate is in our foreheads. But the time has come; the revelation has already occurred, and the guardian seers have seen the lightning strike the darkness we call reality. And now we sleep in the brief interval between the lightning and the thunder.

ACKNOWLEDGMENTS

For his comments and perceptive criticism of the earlier drafts of this book, I would like to express my gratitude to my colleague at York University, Paul Levine. And for his suggestions and general help with publication, I would like to express my thanks to Whitney Blake.

To my wife, Gail, I would like to express my deepest appreciation, for from a winter's chilblains in an uncentrally heated flat in Dublin to heat prostration from summer in Yucatán, she has never complained about the wandering the books have entailed, but has always faithfully complained when the books themselves deserved it, and so has put as much of her life into them as I have.

To the Trustees of the Old Dominion Foundation, I wish to express my gratitude for the fellowship that began the project which ended with this book. To Professor Richard M. Douglas of M.I.T., I wish to express my thanks for his sponsorship for a grant I received from the Jaspar Whiting Foundation of Boston. And to the Faculty of Arts of York University, I wish to express my gratitude for the summer grants-in-aid which have helped me carry this project to its completion.

NOTES

Chapter 1

LOOKING FOR HISTORY IN L.A.

1. Richard M. Elman, *Ill-At-Ease in Compton* (New York, 1967), p. 4.
2. R. D. Laing, *The Politics of Experience* (New York, 1967), p. 11.
3. Kenneth Boulding, "The Death of the City: A Frightened Look at Post-Civilization," in *The Historian and the City* (Cambridge, 1965).
4. Kevin Lynch, *The Image of the City* (Cambridge, 1960), p. 4.
5. Werner Heisenberg, "The Representation of Nature in Contemporary Physics," in *Symbolism*, ed. Rollo May (New York, 1963).
6. Nathanael West, *The Day of the Locust* (New York, 1950), p. 78.
7. Thomas Pynchon, *The Crying of Lot 49* (New York, 1967), p. 44.
8. Christopher Rand, *Los Angeles: The Ultimate City* (New York, 1966), p. 195.

Chapter 3

GETTING BACK TO THINGS AT M.I.T.

1. *Newsweek* (April 18, 1968, p. 106) has reported the results of a survey of psychiatrists working with the Cape Kennedy engineers and their families. To be fair to the engineers, I should point out that the pattern of successful man but failed father and husband is true for the professional classes generally. Professors of English can be as bad as lawyers, doctors, or engineers in this respect. When I presented part of the material of this chapter at a staff conference at the Langley Porter Neuropsychiatric Hospital in San Francisco, many of the psychiatrists commented that "the aerospace syndrome" was very marked in the professional communities around Berkeley and San Francisco.

2. See La Mont C. Cole's "Can the Earth Be Saved?" in the *New York Times Magazine*, March 31, 1968, p. 35. Also Barry Commoner's *Science and Survival* (New York, 1967) and David Ehrlich, "The Death of the Oceans," in *Ramparts*, September, 1969. Since La Mont C. Cole's *New York Times* essay, a flood of books on ecology has hit the market, but *The Environmental Handbook*, ed. Garrett de Bell, seems to have become a textbook.

3. Albert Rosenfield, *The Second Genesis: The Coming Control of Life*, (Englewood Cliffs, 1969).

4. *Playboy*, September, 1968, p. 224.

5. Werner Heisenberg, "The Representation of Nature in Contemporary Physics," in *Symbolism*, ed. Rollo May (New York, 1963), p. 215

6. Otto Piene remarked on the restraining quality of the nineteenth-century frame at the M.I.T. symposium.

7. Robert Graves and Raphael Patai, *Hebrew Myths: The Book of Genesis* (New York, 1963).

8. Louis Kampf, "The Scandal of Literary Scholar-

ship," in *The Dissenting Academy*, ed. Theodore Roszak (New York, 1968).

9. Noam Chomsky, "A Review of B. F. Skinner's *Verbal Behavior*," in *The Structure of Language*, ed. Fodor and Katz (Englewood Cliffs, 1964).

10. Louis Kampf, *op. cit.*

11. Louis Kampf, *On Modernism* (Cambridge, 1967), p. 218.

Chapter 4

VALUES AND CONFLICT THROUGH HISTORY:

the view from a Canadian retreat

1. William Kilbourn, *Canada: A Guide to the Peaceabl Kingdom* (Toronto, 1970).

2. Claude Lévi-Strauss, *The Savage Mind* (Chicago, 1966).

3. W. B. Yeats, *A Vision* (New York, 1956). The model I am using is a variation of Yeats's, and, moreover, a great simplification. With its twenty-six personality types and its highly complex system of doubled twin opposing forces, the many parameters and variables of the Yeatsian model make it infinitely superior to the present simplification. Its immediate superiority is that it relates structural roles in society to twenty-six different personality types, whereas my simplified model only expresses structural roles. A person can play shaman in one context only to be forced into the role of headman in another. In spite of the superiority of Yeats's *Vision*, I feel justified in offering my sociological simplification because literary critics have considered *A Vision* to be merely a necessary evil in explicating the poems, but otherwise the occult aberration of a brilliant artist. Yeats's philosophy is part of the great

underground tradition which goes back through Blake, Newton, Boehme, and Heraclitus and becomes lost in the darkness of our ignorance of the past. Interestingly enough, those critics who overlook the role of *A Vision* in Yeats's thought are very much of the same mind with those who fail to see that Newton's mysticism was an inseparable part of his Pythagorean science. Since industrial science is now at its point of widest expansion, and Pythagorean science is at its narrowest, it may be worthwhile to notice the similarities of Yeats's occult thought to the more widely recognized work of Werner Heisenberg. Compare, for example, the similarity of the following point of Yeats's with Heisenberg's concept of limit as expressed above on page 61: ". . . When the new gyre begins to stir, I am filled with excitement. I think of recent mathematical research; even the ignorant can compare it with that of Newton—so plainly of the 19th phase —with its objective world intelligible to intellect; I can recognize *that the limit itself has become a new dimension* [my italics], that this ever-hidden thing which makes us fold our hands has begun to press down upon multitudes. Having bruised their hands upon that limit, men, for the first time since the seventeenth century, see the world as an object of contemplation, not as something to be remade [this is prophetic, given the ecological crisis no one was aware of forty years ago when Yeats wrote this], and some few, meeting the limit in their special study, even doubt if there is any common experience, doubt the possibility of science." *A Vision*, p. 300. This criticism of "scientific materialism" should also be compared with Whitehead's *Science and the Modern World*. Appropriately enough for Yeats's synchronous view of history, his remarks were written in Capri in February of 1925, the very year and month in which Whitehead was making similar remarks in his Lowell Lectures at Harvard.

4. Pitirim Sorokin, *Society, Culture and Personality* (New York, 1962), p. 345.

5. Marshall McLuhan, *Understanding Media* (New York, 1965), p. 34.

6. Karl Polanyi, *The Great Transformation* (Boston, 1957), p. 77.

7. Harvey Cox, *The Secular City* (New York, 1965).

8. Sigmund Freud, *Civilization and Its Discontents* (New York, 1961), p. 92.

9. Gordon Rattray-Taylor, *The Biological Time-Bomb* (London, 1968).

10. Kenneth Boulding, in *The Meaning of the Twentieth Century: The Great Transition* (New York, 1964), calls this new culture "post-civilization."

11. Toronto *Daily Star,* May 22, 1969, p. 7.

12. B. F. Skinner, *Walden Two* (New York, 1956), p. 300.

13. Pierre Teilhard de Chardin, *The Future of Man* (New York, 1964), pp. 130, 132.

14. Ivan Illich, *New York Review of Books,* October 9, 1969, p. 12.

For aficionados of Pythagoreanism, I would like to offer the following elabortion of the model of self and civilization:

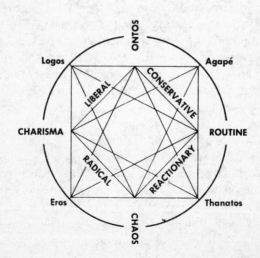

THE FOUR PHASES
  I. Tribal Community: generalized charisma
  II. Agricultural Society: from individuals to institutions
III. Industrial Civilization: from institutions to corporate systems
  IV. Scientific-Planetary Civilization: the individual as institution

"If we review the course of human history we can recognize certain crucial thresholds, the crossing of which has led us to progressively fuller possibilities of life. Among the more prominent of these are the invention and adoption of farming, the achievement of literacy and city life, and in recent times the industrial and scientific revolutions." Grahame Clark, *Stone Age Hunters* (London, 1967), p. 13.

THE FOUR FACULTIES WITH THEIR
FOUR MODES OF CONSCIOUSNESS
Quadrant One: Daimon, with mode of Agapé
Quadrant Two: Body, with mode of Thanatos
Quadrant Three: Heart, with mode of Eros
Quadrant Four: Reason, with mode of Logos

THE FOUR MEDIATIONS OF
THE MODES OF CONSCIOUSNESS:
ONTOS, CHAOS, ROUTINE AND CHARISMA
  The mediation of Logos and Agapé creates Ontos (being). In the mandala this is expressed as a triangle or gyre which is at its widest at the base of Logos-Ontos-Agapé, but winds down to nothing as it turns into the point of its opposite, Chaos (nonbeing). The mediation of Logos and Eros creates Charisma. This is expressed as a triangle which is at its widest at the base of Logos-Charisma-Eros, but winds down to nothing as it turns into the point of its opposite, Routine. Routine is the mediation of Agapé and Thanatos, which is expressed by the gyre which is at its widest at Agapé-Routine-Thanatos, but winds down to nothing as it turns into the point of its opposite, Charisma. Chaos is the mediation of Eros and Thanatos, which is at its widest at

the base of Eros-Chaos-Thanatos, but winds down to nothing as it turns into the point of its opposite at Ontos.

THE FOUR VALUE ORIENTATIONS

If one relates Ontos and Routine, a gyre is created which winds down to nothing as it turns into its opposite in the point of Eros. This triangle expresses the Conservative value orientation. If one relates Chaos and Routine, a gyre is created which winds down to nothing as it turns into its opposite in the point of Logos. This is the Reactionary value orientation. If one relates Chaos and Charisma, a gyre is created which winds down to nothing as it turns into its opposite in the point of Agapé. This is the Radical value orientation. If one relates Charisma and Ontos, a gyre is created which winds down to nothing as it turns into its opposite in the point of Thanatos. This is the Liberal value orientation.

The lines and triangles of the model enable one to see that both Conservatives and Liberals meet at the point of Ontos. Liberals and Radicals meet at the point of Charisma. Radicals and Reactionaries meet at the point of Chaos, and Reactionaries and Conservatives meet at the point of Routine.

As one gazes at the mandala with its four major equilateral triangles, its four isosceles triangles, and its four inscribed squares, he can see that there are other descriptive possibilities to the model. It would help in visualizing the form if it were created in three dimensions with colored neon tubes pulsating with the lights that could express all the possible dynamic relationships between the triangles and the inscribed squares. Needless to say, this is not possible in a literary form. I don't understand all the Pythagorean implications of the model, for being a very poor geometer, this is not my natural way of thinking. Since things like this enter the imagination through a process that Blake liked to call dictation, it is quite possible for an individual to express archetypal forms that he, as a limited person, cannot fully understand.

Chapter 5

A.D. 2000: THE MILLENNIUM UNDER
NEW MANAGEMENT

1. "Toward the Year 2000: Work in Progress," *Daedalus,* Journal of the American Academy of Arts and Sciences, Vol. 96, No. 3 (Summer, 1967), 930–935.
2. *Ibid.,* p. 673.
3. *Ibid.,* p. 686.
4. Jacques Ellul, *The ·Technological Society* (New York, 1967).
5. *Daedalus, op. cit.,* p. 864.
6. *Ibid.,* p. 867.
7. *Ibid.,* p. 821
8. *Ibid.,* p. 965.
9. Herman Kahn and Anthony J. Weiner, *The Year 2000: A Framework for Speculation on the Next Thirty-Three Years* (New York, 1967), p. 7.
10. *Ibid.,* pp. 211–212.
11. Norman Cohn, *The Pursuit of the Millennium* (New York, 1961).
12. Kahn and Weiner, *op. cit.,* p. 277.
13. A. F. C. Wallace, "Revitalization Movements," *American Anthropologist,* Vol. LVIII (April, 1956), 264–281.
14. Kahn and Weiner, *op. cit.,* pp. 346 f. My italics. This picture of damaged brains linked to computers represents, I think, the grossest form of comic-book science fiction masquerading as scientific prediction. Whenever in history scientists are coming to the top of a mountain, it looks to them as if the stars were resting on the peaks, and so they declaim and declaim how everything is just about wrapped up. So it was with Rutherford and atomic physics at the turn of the century, and so it is now with Marvin Minsky and "artificial intelligence." But as Lévi-

Strauss has remarked: "And when we do finally succeed in understanding life as a function of inert matter, it will be to discover that the latter has properties very different from those previously attributed to it." (*The Savage Mind,* p. 247.) To write my own science fiction in opposition to Kahn and Weiner, I would say that the macroscopic models of superconducters as single quantum states will provide specific physical content for Whitehead's metaphysical structures, and that just as the superconductor eliminates resistance in the crystal lattice and creates a fantastic supraorganic unity, so matter in the brain will be seen to function entirely differently from atoms in inert matter. By the year 2000, then I think the statements of Kahn and Weiner, as well as those of B. F. Skinner and Marvin Minsky, will appear as ridiculous as similar statements made about human machines in the seventeenth century.

15. Address given to the 38th Annual Couchiching Conference, Lake Geneva, Ontario, July 29, 1969. Dr. Illich has said that the statement is a paraphrase of a remark by Marx that is very similar to a point made by St. John of the Cross.

16. B. F. Skinner, "The Machine That Is Man," *Psychology Today,* April, 1969, p. 20.

Chapter 6

THE RE-VISIONING OF HISTORY

1. Karl Mannheim, *Ideology and Utopia* (London, 1960), p. 36
2. Jess Stern, *The Sleeping Prophet* (New York, 1967).
3. Louis Pauwels and Jacques Bergier, *The Dawn of Magic* (London, 1963).
4. Sigmund Freud, *The Future of an Illusion* (New York, 1961), p. 21.

5. Northrop Frye, *Fearful Symmetry: A Study of William Blake* (Princeton, 1958), p. 126.

6. Edgar Evans Cayce, *Edgar Cayce on Atlantis* (New York, 1968).

7. Thomas Pynchon, *The Crying of Lot 49* (New York, 1966), p. 98.

8. C. S. Lewis, *Mere Christianity* (London, 1952), p. 52. See also his science fiction trilogy: *Out of the Silent Planet; Perelandra; That Hideous Strength* (New York, 1965).

9. C. S. Lewis, *The Chronicles of Narnia: The Magician's Nephew* (London, 1963), p. 24.

10. D. H. Lawrence, *Fantasia of the Unconscious* (New York, 1960), p. 54.

11. *The Velikovsky Affair,* ed. Alfred de Gracia (New York, 1966).

12. Jess Stern, *op. cit.,* p. 223.

13. Allen Spraggett, Toronto *Daily Star,* February 18, 1969, p. 7.

14. J. Manson Valentine, "The Discovery and Possible Significance of X Kukican, Ancient Maya Site," Alabama Museum of Natural History, February, 1965.

15. J. Manson Valentine, "Archaeological Enigmas of Florida and the Western Bahamas," *Museum News,* Museum of Science, Miami, Florida, Vol. 1, No. 2 (June, 1969).

16. Charles Hapgood, *Maps of the Ancient Sea Kings: Evidence of Advanced Civilization in the Ice Age* (Philadelphia, 1966), pp. 193, 194.

17. Giorgio de Santillana and Hertha von Dechend, *Hamlet's Mill: An Essay on Myth and the Frame of Time* (Boston, 1969).

18. Loren Eiseley, *The Immense Journey* (New York, 1956), p. 86.

19. As quoted in Eiseley, p. 94.

20. Charles Hockett and Robert Aschar, "The Human Revolution," *Current Anthropology,* Vol. 5 (1964), pp. 135–147.

21. Noam Chomsky, *Language and Mind* (New York, 1968), pp. 59, 83.
22. Claude Lévi-Strauss, *Tristes Tropiques* (New York, 1963), pp. 233, 275.
23. Grahame Clark, *Stone Age Hunters* (London, 1967), p. 13.
24. V. Gordon Childe, *Man Makes Himself* (Suffolk, 1965).
25. James Mellaart, *Çatal Hüyük: A Neolithic Town in Anatolia* (London, 1967).
26. Michale D. Coe, *America's First Civilization: Discovering the Olmec* (New York, 1968), p. 127.
27. Claude Lévi-Strauss, *The Savage Mind* (Chicago, 1966), p. 15.
28. V. Gordon Childe, *op. cit.*, p. 226.
29. Michael Coe, *op. cit.*, p. 127.
30. *Ibid.*, p. 117.
31. Delia Goetz, Sylvanus G. Morley, and Adrián Recinos, *The Popol Vuh* (Norman, 1950), p. 172.
32. Alfred M. Tozzer, *Landa's Relación de las coasas de Yucatán*, Papers of the Peabody Museum (Cambridge, 1941), p. 16.
33. Frank Waters, *Boko of the Hopi* (New York, 1969), p. 26.
34. Miguel Leon-Portilla, *Pre-Columbian Literatures of Mexico* (Norman, 1969), p. 119.
35. Erich von Daniken, *Chariots of the Gods?* (London, 1969); Francis Mazière, *Mysteries of Easter Island* (London, 1969).
36. Leon Festinger et al., *When Prophecy Fails* (New York, 1964). See also Robert Wauchope, *Lost Tribes and Sunken Continents* (Chicago, 1964), and also Peter Worsley, *The Trumpet Shall Sound: A Study of Cargo Cults in Melanesia* (New York, 1968). A cargo cult is a messianic movement in which the natives prepare for the return of the gods who are to bring with them a sacred cargo that will solve all problems.

37. M. I. Finley, *New York Review of Books,* May 22, 1969, p. 38.

38. J. V. Luce, *The End of Atlantis: New Light on an Old Legend* (London, 1969).

39. W. F. Albright, *The Biblical Period from Abraham to Ezra* (New York, 1963), p. 1.

40. Robert Graves and Raphael Patai, *Hebrew Myths: The Book of Genesis* (New York, 1963), p. 113.

41. S. N. Kramer, *The Sumerians: Their History, Culture, and Character* (Chicago, 1963), p. 33.

42. *The Book of Enoch,* ed. R. H. Charles (Oxford, 1912), p. 35.

43. T. S. Kuhn, *The Structure of Scientific Revolution* (New York, 1962), pp. 6, 111.

44. Arthur C. Clarke, *The City and the Stars* (New York, 1953), p. 101.

45. *Ibid.,* pp. 256, 264.

46. *Ibid.*

47. W. B. Yeats, "The Supernatural Songs," in *Collected Poems* (New York, 1957), p. 287.

48. Thomas Sugrue, *There Is a River: The Story of Edgar Cayce* (New York, 1967), p. 312.

49. Irene Nicholson, *Mexican and Central American Mythology* (London, 1967), p. 312. See also Laurette Sejourné, *Burning Water: Thought and Religion in Ancient Mexico* (London, 1957), p. 123, for a description of man's entry into the world through the sacred tree of Tamoanchán. The relevant lines from Blake are from "The Human Abstract":

> *The Gods of the earth and sea*
> *Sought thro' Nature to find this Tree;*
> *But their search was all in vain:*
> *There grows one in the Human Brain.*

Adam and Eve stand beside a tree around which a snake is coiled, and on top of which a special kind of fruit flowers. The Sumerian hero Gilgamesh tries to chop down a tree for the goddess of love,

Inanna, in which a snake is coiled; however, he finds he cannot cut the tree because the zu bird has made its nest on the top of the tree. In the Temple of the Foliated Cross at Palenque, Mexico, the Maya relief shows two men beside a tree, a beast at the base of the tree, and a quetzal bird on top. I believe that the spinal column is esoterically represented in all of these iconographic traditions, be they Sumerian, Hebrew, Hindu, Hopi, or Maya. To raise the serpent of kundalini until it touches the brain and causes the "thousand-petaled lotus" to flower is, on Mexican terms, to teach the serpent how to fly. The iridescent Plumed Serpent of archaic Mexico and the multicolored coronal chakra of Indian Yoga are the same. The evolutionists, as opposed to the diffusionists, would say that because the human mind is everywhere true to form, similarities occur in all cultures. I can believe that light and dark symbolism will occur in all religions, but I find it hard to believe that independent cultures will develop similar esoteric systems and iconography. I find it much easier to suspect that an *Urkultur* is behind the similarities in Sumerian, Egyptian, Hebrew, Greek, Indian, Hopi, and Maya symbolism.

50. Arthur C. Clark, *2001: A Space Odyssey* (New York, 1968), p. vii.

51. *Soviet and East European Abstracts Series,* University of Glasgow, July, 1970, p. 52. See also *Extraterrestrial Civilizations,* ed. G. M. Tovmasyan, Israel Program for Scientific Translations (Jerusalem, 1967). In this symposium, V. A. Ambartsumyan of Byurakan Astrophysical Observatory says: "We have no doubt whatsoever that life and civilizations exist on a multitude of celestial bodies." (P. 3.) The American equivalent is Walter Sullivan's *We Are not Alone: The Search for Intelligent Life On Other Worlds* (New York, 1964).

52. Arthur C. Clarke, *2001.* p. 175.

INDEX